'Few leaders can boast to have led through [industry] industry events over the past 40 years. Ste[ve] PC, the networking era, the internet, mobil[e] AI. If you want to learn how to effectively navigate through massive change, this book is for you.'

— **David Shein, general partner, OIF VC**

'Steve distils his lifetime experience in major organisations at the technological frontier. It isn't the "tech" that interests him rather people and what they can achieve with the right motivation, support and work culture. This book provides a powerful case for change and a practical and compelling guide to action.'

— **Emeritus Professor Roy Green AM**

'Steve Vamos has packed in so much practical wisdom into Shifts and Shocks drawn from his depth of global business experience. This makes Shifts and Shocks an essential guide for anyone in leadership.'

— **Narelle Hooper, award-winning Australian business editor and interviewer (Company Director, AFR BOSS Magazine), non-executive director The Ethics Centre**

'Whether you are a CEO of a large listed company or a team member of a small start-up, the "Must-dos" Steve recommends can help every industry, business and team change better to achieve their full potential.'

— **Clinical Professor Leanne Rowe AM**

'After seeing Steve speak years ago, it was humbling to meet one of my heroes and have him help shape Xero to be a global technology business. It has also been humbling to be a peer to Steve, and to become over many shared experiences and laughs, a friend.'

— **Rod Drury, founder, Xero**

'Steve Vamos succeeded in doing what very few executives have accomplished in the tech industry: taking the reins of a high-growth, industry-defining company from its iconic founder/CEO and taking it to the next level. Whatever Steve has to say about that amazing journey deserves our attention and admiration.'

— **Graham Smith, former board chair, Splunk and Xero**

THROUGH
SHIFTS
AND
SHOCKS

Lessons from the Front Line
of Technology and Change

STEVE VAMOS

Global executive from Xero, Microsoft and Apple

WILEY

First published 2025 by John Wiley & Sons Australia, Ltd

ISBN: 978-1-394-29350-6

A catalogue record for this book is available from the National Library of Australia

Registered Office
John Wiley & Sons Australia, Ltd. Level 4, 600 Bourke Street, Melbourne, VIC 3000, Australia

For details of our global editorial offices, customer services, and more information about Wiley products visit us at www.wiley.com.

Cover design by Wiley
Cover image: © Rolling Stones/Adobe Stock

Set in Warnock Pro 11/15pt by Straive, Chennai, India
SKY48BFAB95-2D44-4598-AE35-C68B599E02C0_111524

For my father, Peter Vamos

CONTENTS

Part IV: Take action and be rewarded   175

INTRODUCTION

We are living at a time defined by constant and accelerating change, which gives rise to two big problems that need to be solved, and solved fast:

- Problem 1. Our ability to lead and respond to change is not good enough (to put it kindly).

- Problem 2. Change is best managed through great teamwork and collaboration, yet most people work in mediocre teams, limiting their ability to perform at their best.

These problems lead to flawed or failed change initiatives, wasted human potential and low productivity. The resulting social and economic impacts on the wellbeing of people, organisations and societies are significant and unacceptable.

So how do we fix it? By improving the way leaders and members of their teams think and act in the face of change. This can be any kind of change such as responding to external forces, improving a product or process, or taking action to help teams work better together.

We must urgently address this problem of wasted potential and productivity in the workplace by learning how to be better at change.

Organisations don't change unless their people do, and without the right approach to engaging people and teams, the status quo outweighs the change agenda every day and progress stalls.

Despite successive waves of hype around new technology, it isn't technology doing the disrupting; it's people! Technology amplifies the potential of people. But at the same time as being the force behind change, people also offer the greatest resistance to it. Change is hard for people because our natural reaction to it is shaped by:

- fear — an important instinctive response to change
- conditioning — from our social and workplace influences
- attachment — to past success and knowledge.

Now more than ever, the human element of change must be a constant, front-of-mind obsession and focus of attention on any change journey.

In this book I share the most important things about leading, responding to and overcoming the human challenge of change that I have learned from 40 years on the front line of the technology industry. I also share the most effective tools I use to enable people and teams to perform at their best in the face of change.

Change is a human thing more than a technology thing, so being good at it requires focus on *who you need to be* and *what you need to do* to make change happen better.

The right place at the worst time

I know what being disrupted feels like. I've been at the right places at the worst times throughout my career, from being the CEO of software company Xero during the COVID-19 pandemic to experiencing crises at IBM, Apple and ninemsn. I am a survivor from the front line of virtually every significant shift and shock to the technology sector and industry over the last 40 years.

Figure I.1, a snapshot of my professional journey through four decades, shows the shifts of change impacting computing, technology and society, and the shocks of disruptive industry, economic and global events.

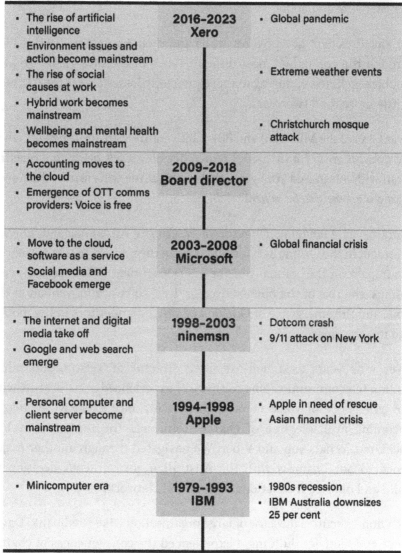

SHIFTS   **SHOCKS**

SHIFTS		SHOCKS
• The rise of artificial intelligence • Environment issues and action become mainstream • The rise of social causes at work • Hybrid work becomes mainstream • Wellbeing and mental health becomes mainstream	**2016–2023** **Xero**	• Global pandemic • Extreme weather events • Christchurch mosque attack
• Accounting moves to the cloud • Emergence of OTT comms providers: Voice is free	**2009–2018** **Board director**	
• Move to the cloud, software as a service • Social media and Facebook emerge	**2003–2008** **Microsoft**	• Global financial crisis
• The internet and digital media take off • Google and web search emerge	**1998–2003** **ninemsn**	• Dotcom crash • 9/11 attack on New York
• Personal computer and client server become mainstream	**1994–1998** **Apple**	• Apple in need of rescue • Asian financial crisis
• Minicomputer era	**1979–1993** **IBM**	• 1980s recession • IBM Australia downsizes 25 per cent

Figure I.1: career chronology shifts and shocks

Back in the early 1990s, as General Manager of IBM's Western Australia branch, I announced the company's first-ever layoffs in Australia. The announcement ended the longstanding ideal of 'jobs for life' at IBM, the giant of the mainframe computer era that dominated the information technology industry for decades. The layoffs, which were called a 'voluntary relocation program', were hardly voluntary, as offers of alternative roles in Sydney or Canberra were generally unpalatable to our Perth-based people.

As Vice President of Apple Australia and then Apple Asia Pacific, I led through the company's most difficult times in the mid 1990s. Apple's troubles included enduring massive quarterly losses and three CEOs in a little more than two years.

I was CEO of the Microsoft and PBL joint-venture start-up, ninemsn, when the dotcom crash hit in 2000. I remember how it felt being in a meeting room with a hundred young people looking at me with fear in their eyes, asking me, *where to from here?*

Working as Managing Director of Microsoft Australia, and as Vice President in the Online Services Division in the mid 2000s, I experienced the impact on the company of the US Department of Justice anti-trust rulings, the rise of the open-source or 'free' software movement at the time, and the emergence of Google and other competitors in the mobile and internet space.

Over nine years as a non-executive director of Telstra, Australia's leading telecommunications company, I experienced a major shift with the emergence of voice messaging services, once exclusive to telcos, becoming available free of charge from 'over the top' services like FaceTime, WhatsApp and Viber. We navigated through another major shock to our business with the Australian government's decision to build and operate the National Broadband Network.

As a non-executive director of large organisations like Medibank, David Jones and Fletcher Building, I experienced the consequences of change and technology disruption in the health insurance, department store retail, and building products and construction industries.

Leading Xero, a fast-growing global technology business, through the pandemic required me to lean on every bit of learning from experience I had gained about confronting change and uncertain circumstances.

Despite the unique nature of the pandemic (I hadn't managed through one of those before), I felt clear and confident about how I needed to be and what I needed to do to guide our business through the challenge. That's not to say I always got things right or executed as well as I'd have liked. Facing into change and uncertainty is not the domain of perfection; it is about learning as quickly as you can and correcting course as you go.

During those long days, weeks and months working from my apartment in Wellington, New Zealand, I was thankful for the people and experience that had shaped me and prepared me for what I had to face.

Who is this book for?

This book is intended to help anyone who wants their team to perform better, their work environment to improve or the change initiatives they are part of to succeed. In an immediate and practical sense, people who lead organisations and teams will gain most, because they have the greatest influence on the nature of teamwork and the success of change initiatives.

However, any individual contributor can also use the actions and tools to encourage and help the leader of their team improve performance. Individual team members can have a very positive influence on performance especially if their team leader is receptive.

Whatever your aspirations are for a better future in whatever domain you care about, the superpower you must develop is how to effectively lead and respond to change.

> *Whatever the change being initiated or confronted, at work or in life,* **Through Shifts and Shocks** *will help anyone improve the change process they are working on.*

How this book can help

This book takes you on a journey, from exploring the nature of change, and why change is so hard, through to how you can best think and act in the face of change.

Part I looks at how technology has amplified the potential of people, and trends that are changing the nature of our workplaces, and at why change is hard for humans.

Part II explains how you need to think and behave to be your best in leading change and building a great team, and how having the right mindset, self-awareness and care for people is critical.

Part III covers the most important things that must be done to drive change, execute strategy and build a great team, and how to do that by confronting difficult conversations and making hard choices.

Part IV outlines how to make effective change and great teamwork happen. This section includes a diagnostic, playbooks and tools that have served me well over the years. You will also find playbooks that can help individual contributors and Board Directors take appropriate action.

Finally, I reflect on the rewards of doing the hard work of being a leader of change and great teams. For me, one reward has been the opportunity to work with talented people, especially those who have shown appreciation for how I have helped their career and development. I also reflect on the reward of learning from and observing up close high-profile technology industry leaders, including Xero founder Rod Drury, Australian media and entertainment giants James and Kerry Packer, Microsoft co-founder Bill Gates, Steve Ballmer and Apple co-founder Steve Jobs.

Two domains and eight Must-Do actions

Two domains, 'Being' and 'Doing', frame the eight Must-Do actions in the book:

- **Being** reflects the important character attributes of a leader and team, such as self-awareness and having the right mindset and motivation, when initiating or confronting change.

- **Doing** reflects the words spoken and actions taken to execute change by confronting difficult conversations, making hard choices, seeking clarity, driving alignment and focusing on performance.

Great change and teamwork come down to activating across these two domains.

Across the two domains of Being and Doing, eight Must-Do actions, listed in figure I.2, represent the most important lessons I've learned and applied. The eight Must-Do actions cut through the expansive volume of things to consider about leadership, teamwork and change in order to focus on the actions that deliver the most benefit.

	Must-Do actions
BEING *Character*	1. Apply the <u>right mindset</u>
	2. Be <u>self-aware</u>
	3. <u>Care about people</u>
DOING *Words and actions*	4. Seek <u>clarity</u>
	5. Drive <u>alignment</u>
	6. Focus on <u>performance</u>
	7. <u>Have difficult conversations</u>
	8. <u>Make hard choices</u>

Figure I.2: the two domains and eight Must-Do actions

The Must-Do actions are interconnected. For example, if you don't *apply the right mindset,* progress on all other Must-Dos will be limited. And, it will be hard to *drive alignment* if you don't *have difficult conversations.*

No individual or team is great at all Must-Dos at once. External circumstances (such as a global pandemic) and internal circumstances (such as a change of team members) will impact progress.

Understanding current performance and continuously improving in any of the Must-Dos will have a positive impact on the quality of change efforts and teamwork. The aim is not to seek perfection; it is to understand your current reality and drive small improvements every day to gain the associated benefits.

The change journey for any person, leader or team is analogous to sailing between two locations, correcting course as wind conditions change. The journey towards your intended destination is rarely travelled in a straight line.

Are you up for what follows reading this book?

The eight Must-Dos are largely common sense, but that doesn't make them common practice or easy to do. If they were easy, many more organisations would be high performing and envied, and many more change programs would succeed.

The Must-Dos are hard to execute because they require having difficult, confronting conversations, making hard choices and taking actions that are tough to execute because of their impact on people close to you.

At Xero, I would meet with people across our business and ask them one question: 'What's the one thing about Xero you would change if you were the CEO?' I was open to hearing the truth and confronting uncomfortable reality, so I lived every day with the knowledge and frustration that the Xero I wanted us to be was not the Xero our people experienced every day.

This dissatisfaction is not unique to me and Xero but is an aspect of the culture of the technology industry that is common to most of the companies I have worked with (although not necessarily under all leaders). We would force ourselves to see the gap between current reality and aspiration and work hard to close it. It is a culture that doesn't spend much time celebrating success; rather, it quickly notes progress and moves on to the next challenge.

Your level of commitment and accountability to close the gap between current reality and your aspirations (and those of people around you) is unique to you. It comes down to what motivates you and how much you care about helping others around you to be more successful (or appreciate the extent to which your success is enabled by this).

I never shoot for perfection; I gave up on that a long time ago. Instead, I shoot for better every day. The exciting thing is that people see it, feel it and thank you for it, even if you're still some distance from where you want to be, because it means a lot to their work lives and how they feel about what they are doing.

> *For this book to be as useful to you as I want it to be, the question you need to answer is: How committed are you to prioritise and take action every day that will change things for the better for those around you?*

If you commit to working every day to execute improvement in any Must-Do, you will build a more successful organisation or team, one that can change better and perform better — I guarantee it!

I hope *Through Shifts and Shocks* will be the most useful business book you'll read and that it contributes to greater success for you at work and in life.

PART I

WHAT HAS CHANGED AND WHY CHANGE IS HARD

'Shifts and shocks' characterise the rapid evolution of technology and its impact on people and the course of every industry. As one wave of technology enables and gives way to the next, more change and disruption follow.

Artificial intelligence, blockchain and the metaverse have played into recent waves of technological change that have grabbed attention. For a time we are caught up in the hype and debate about how each innovation will change the nature of work and life. I can be a bit of a sceptic. In the 1980s the hype was all about the 'paperless office', and I'm still waiting, but that's only part of the reason I'm sceptical.

The truth is that in the short term the hype rarely lives up to expectation, yet with time almost every wave of significant new technology has created long-term change in how we work, live and play. 'Convergence' of text, data and media was the talk for decades, until 2007 when the stars aligned and Apple delivered the iPhone.

The more significant reason to downplay the hype around technology is that the real story of technology change is a *human* story. As new services emerge that make doing things easier and cheaper, it is people putting technology to use that is the source of change. Technology is the enabler.

At the same time as being the source of change, people are also the source of *resistance* to change. Some technology has taken decades to be fully embraced and adopted.

As a case in point, the adoption of cloud accounting software by small business has a long way to run around the world despite having been successfully embraced by millions over the past 10 to 12 years.

Technology change doesn't happen without people changing. After observing this in many different contexts over 40 years, I strongly believe this:

Change is a human thing more than a technology thing.

And the more technology surrounds and enables us, the more the human element matters. In Part I we look at the human nature of change, what has changed and why change is so challenging for people.

CHAPTER 1

TECHNOLOGY AMPLIFIES PEOPLE!

Technology amplifies the value and potential of people, requiring us to think differently and more deliberately about the human element of everything we do.

People are our greatest asset!

We often hear leaders of organisations say this, but how often have you really felt or believed it? In some cases (if you're lucky) it plays out in action rather than just talk, but more often the reality falls short. Despite that, much research has confirmed that people and the value they create are indeed our greatest asset, and it's time to embrace that principle with conviction.

Figure 1.1 (overleaf) plots the dramatic shift in the proportion of enterprise value (using the S&P 500 as a benchmark) from physical and financial assets to those often referred to as 'intangible' or 'other factors'.

Physical and financial business value (the stuff you can touch or count) has dropped from 68 per cent in 1985 to just 10 per cent of total market value in 2020.

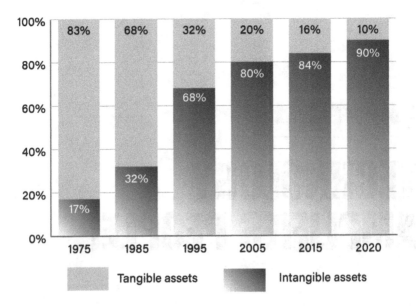

Figure 1.1: S&P market value

Source: Ocean Tomo

Intangible value (stuff that's hard to touch or count directly) reflects human knowledge, relationships and potential, in the form of goodwill and brand value.

No wonder share prices are volatile. With 90 per cent of value tied up in what we can't touch or count, it is understandable that when an organisation or the economy experiences uncertainty or a shock of any kind, investors flee and market values plummet. For example, according to CNBC the big tech companies Apple, Microsoft, Google, Amazon and Facebook lost a combined US $1.3 trillion of their market value between 19 February 2020 and 23 March 2020, when the global pandemic hit.

It's sobering to realise that most of the value of a business derives from an expectation that the people in the organisation will continue to create value from their intellectual property, ideas and actions well into the future.

We have well-established measurement and assurance processes for financial and physical assets; the same can't be said for intangibles or the human elements of value creation.

Financial performance reporting is a bit like looking at the light from a distant star. What you see today is an outcome of what happened in the past, rather than how today's reality will play out in the future.

Management and measurement of the 'non-financial value drivers' (often demeaned as 'soft' measures), such as staff engagement and customer satisfaction surveys, are now more commonly used to monitor performance. The Employee Net Promoter Score (eNPS) is one example and a meaningful element of compensation incentives for senior leaders at Xero.

Integrated Reporting, initially stewarded by the International Integrated Reporting Committee (IIRC), is increasingly demanded by shareholders and embraced by corporate Boards. This momentum is also reflected in additional environmental reporting standards, such as the Task Force on Climate-related Financial Disclosures (TCFD), the Global Reporting Initiative (GRI) and organisations such as the Sustainability Accounting Standards Board (SASB), which publicly listed companies increasingly observe and need to comply with.

This reporting aims to provide better insights into longer-term business prospects across a range of dimensions, with varying levels of interest from a wide range of stakeholders.

Given how valuations increasingly recognise that 'people are our greatest asset', we need to place far more emphasis on the human and relationship elements of performance.

Despite increasing use of top-level eNPS or employee engagement scores for the human element of organisational performance, stakeholders (including boards) have insufficient insight to assess the impact of the human element on organisation performance. This book suggests ways to better address this need going forward.

The potential of people is amplified

As noted, digital technology has changed many industries by amplifying the impact of their people. Consider the customer and shareholder value created by top internet services such as Amazon, Airbnb, Uber and WhatsApp, to mention just a few. The same is evident across many other industries.

Information and communications technology has provided us with access to more information and knowledge than ever before. It has allowed us to connect and share with others more than ever before. For these reasons, the potential value of people to the organisations they work for has greatly increased.

When I started work at IBM in 1979, my best sources of information were my dad (a wonderful mentor), my boss, more experienced people around me at work and the trusty if unwieldy *Encyclopaedia Britannica*. I could also count on relevant learning from my university and school education.

Today we have instant access to unlimited sources of knowledge and information thanks to the internet. I guess that's why my daughters never ranked me at the top of their sources of knowledge or information.

Back in the early eighties we didn't have email and rarely spoke to or connected with more than 10 people in a day. These people were physically nearby or available on a local phone call. International communication was achieved by means of a Telex (from a dedicated room staffed by a specialist operator) with the hope of receiving a response in three or four days' time. Today we communicate with people anytime, anywhere, almost instantaneously, to the point that we are all 'media outlets' and have the potential to influence others on a much bigger scale.

Reflecting on these changes, it is important to remember that *technology isn't disrupting you and your business, people are!*

A simple way of looking at the amplified potential value of people is to consider these two dimensions:

- knowledge — what you (or the people in your organisation) know

- relationships — who you (or the people in your organisation) are connected to.

Knowledge and relationships combine to create economic and social value. You need both in order to create the value. If you are the smartest person in the world but don't connect with anyone, you will create no value. If you are the most connected person in the world, but know nothing, again you will create no value. Real value can only be created when knowledge is shared or passed between people.

human potential = knowledge × connection

If you embrace this simple model of human and organisational value being a function of individual and combined knowledge multiplied by connection, then you can see that in each of the past four decades the potential of people and organisations (to do good or bad) has been amplified substantially.

Despite this amplified human potential, many organisational leaders and managers fail to tap into this resource. Productivity and potential are going to waste because we still think and act (often unconsciously) with a limiting mindset that sees people as tools to get things done rather than as hearts and minds that can create new possibilities for organisations.

Young people today are smarter and more connected and have greater expectations than their predecessors. This is because they have far greater access to information and more connections than were possible when baby boomers and Generation X entered the workforce.

Generation Y and Millennials are more motivated by meaningful purpose because they have grown up with more options and sources of information than previous generations. They are less likely to take no for an answer and more likely to search for what they believe does or should exist. This characteristic reflects greater potential that we need to value and engage with.

My daughters' experience entering the workforce convinced me that in some professions, senior people expected young people to suffer the same limited scope of work they did when they started out many years ago. I'm not suggesting that young people shouldn't be 'put through the mill' when it comes to gaining the required professional skills and experience, but rather that if we don't listen to them, value their input and create opportunities for them to contribute beyond basic tasks, we will lose them.

Let's face it, your industry and organisation are most likely to be disrupted by young people outside the organisation, so why not make your own young people disrupters?

Importantly, the same applies to all people, regardless of age and generation. What Gen Y and Millennials want we all wanted too, but we didn't live in a time when it was possible.

We must stop thinking of people and their potential in historic terms or by relating it to our own experience.

> *Underestimating the potential of people is a huge trap. We must think and operate in a way that encourages and enables the people who work with us to be the best they can be.*

There is one further important factor in realising human potential: motivation. Everywhere, around the world, we see social movements arise that take advantage of the potential of people to make change happen. The energy behind their efforts comes from their motivation to make things different from how they were in the past.

Given the importance of motivation to potential and change, the formula is:

$$\text{human potential} = \text{knowledge} \times \text{connection} \times \text{motivation}$$

Organisations are a social network

If you're asked to picture your organisation, there's a good chance you will picture a traditional hierarchical organisation chart with the boss at the top, direct reports underneath and so on down through the hierarchy.

Figure 1.2 is not your organisation. It is a representation of a traditional management hierarchy. The underlying nature of your organisation is a social network of people connecting and interacting with each other.

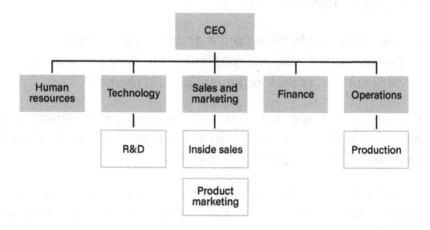

Figure 1.2: traditional organisation chart

Information and communications technology has connected us to one another as never before. So rather than picture a hierarchy, we are much better served thinking about our organisation as a social network with many connections between people inside and outside the organisation, as shown in figure 1.3.

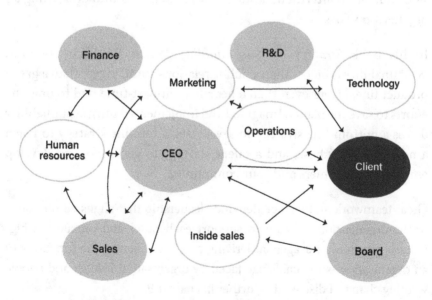

Figure 1.3: social network organisation chart

Organisations have always been networks, but today, with the availability of communication and collaboration tools like Microsoft Teams, Zoom and Google Hangout, those connections are more prolific and instantaneous than ever before.

Leaders need to develop the nodes (people) and connections (relationships) that make up the social network that is their organisation and teams.

The hierarchical and functional silo views of organisations that dominate our thinking are industrial-age representations that block organisational potential and strategy execution.

Not seeing the connected nature of things is a blindness caused by our conditioning to prioritise the tangible (or physical) and undervalue the intangible (or human) aspect of organisational performance.

Our external stakeholders are also networked with us, which further increases our ability to learn from and collaborate with each other. The consequences are significant, including putting external stakeholder needs front and centre of organisation strategy, risk and performance management systems. Corporate social responsibility is no longer a side issue or an afterthought; rather, it is integrated into everything an organisation does.

In his book *Strategy for Sustainability*, Adam Werbach observes, 'Sustainability is bigger than a public relations stunt, bigger than a green product line, bigger even than a heartfelt but part-time nod to ongoing efforts to save the planet. Imagined and implemented fully, sustainability drives a bottom-line strategy to save costs, a top-line strategy to reach a new consumer base, and a talent strategy to get, keep, and develop employees, customers and your community.'

Great teamwork and change demands leadership that aligns all functions of the organisation or team to support each other and pursue the big-picture priorities and agenda. Driving alignment across the functions of an organisation is the challenge faced by organisation leaders and people wanting change. I discuss this further in chapter 9.

Artificial intelligence (AI) is the next amplifier

The rapid adoption of AI tools such as ChatGPT, Google Gemini and Microsoft Copilot represents another big step forward in amplifying human potential. The continuing evolution and application of AI is unstoppable.

One exciting and enabling aspect of AI is that anyone can interact with the AI to 'write a program' without needing to be a software engineer. Another is how AI can accelerate the creative process. When I was trying to decide on a title for this book, I was able to brainstorm with AI and compile a list of hundreds of potential names very quickly. Without AI it would have taken me much longer to come up with far fewer alternatives. The title I finally chose did not come from the AI brainstorm, but the process convinced me the title I selected was the one I wanted.

There's a lot of attention on how AI-enabled applications will impact us. Will more jobs be created than lost? I don't know the answer, but if you look back at previous predictions of how technology would put humans out of work, in the long run new jobs were created to compensate for those lost. Think of the role of the 'prompt engineer', who specialises in asking the right question of the AI, and other roles that validate the output. Some jobs will be eliminated of course, and we will need to look after those who are most impacted.

Before we conclude that software engineers will no longer be needed, we should consider the massive backlog of software applications that exists across the world today. Just as the digital camera dramatically increased the number of photos being taken each day, AI will continue to democratise software development, putting much more of it in the hands of users. Greater engineering capacity will be available to develop more complex applications further down the backlog list, because people will be able to extract insights and information more easily from the data they are interested in.

Speaking of data, the AI revolution increases the need for people and organisations to protect, manage and improve the quality of data they own. The principle of 'garbage in, garbage out' will be a gating factor in how useful AI-generated insights and content will be.

Recently I visited the City Gallery in Wellington, New Zealand, to see artist Reuben Paterson's exhibition 'The Only Dream Left'. I was fortunate to speak with Reuben among a few friends, one of whom decided to demonstrate the benefit of ChatGPT by asking for further information about one of Reuben's works called *David*, a life-size sculpture of a bear. As the results of the search were read out, Reuben identified incorrect references to where 'David' had been on show. AI is only as good as the data it has access to.

Where data quality is good, the potential to use AI to amplify the human element of business relationships is exciting. In many industries the quality of relationships can be improved by using AI to keep in touch with customers and provide enhanced service. The key to being able to do this will be the quality of the actual relationship. My advice to all business owners is to remember that the more things change, the more the fundamentals matter. Do these two things well and you'll have great opportunities to amplify your business in an AI world:

1. Care about the people you do business with, understanding their needs and experience of doing business with you.

2. Treat the data in your business as gold. Invest in the right technology to manage it, and don't give it to anyone else unless you fully understand their intended use of it.

When it comes to exploiting AI, we must be alert to the potential that some people will use it with ill intent, just as we were increasingly concerned about the security of our data when our home computers were connected to the internet in the 1990s. Unfortunately, the potential for people to do bad things is also amplified.

Issues of privacy, security and safety will only become more urgent as AI becomes more powerful and human-centric. In response, regulations and law enforcement will continue to evolve to address these issues.

Finally, the growing uptake in AI usage underscores how change enabled by technology adoption is accelerating, as shown in figure 1.4. For this reason, our capacity to lead and respond to change is only going to become more important. The Must-Dos I discuss throughout the book are the anchors I rely on to meet that need.

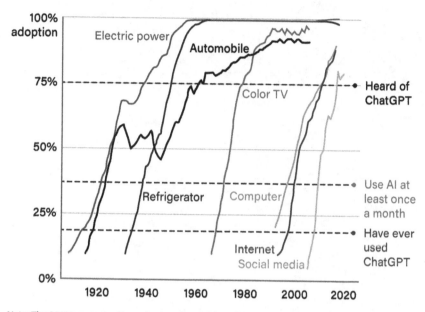

Note: The 2023 survey results are for American adults, while the historical data are for American households.

Figure 1.4: adoption of modern technologies

Source: Our World in Data, Pew Research Center, and YouGov

CHAPTER 2

HUMANS IN A NEW WORLD OF WORK

The global pandemic was a huge shock to our operating environment and served as an unwelcome catalyst for shifts in many domains of work and life.

Positive changes such as the shift to hybrid and more flexible workplaces, and the adoption of technologies that enable them, were accompanied by a greater concern for the wellbeing of people at work and the de-stigmatisation of mental health issues.

Negative consequences, beyond the tragic loss of human life, included the disruption to supply chains, the movement of people and availability of talent. As COVID unwound, the related inflationary effects of these disruptions led to higher interest rates, which had a significant impact on consumers and business. Growth-oriented companies, especially those not generating cash, had to act fast to reduce their workforce.

In this chapter we explore several areas of change that have emerged or become more prominent during and since the pandemic. These include diversity and inclusion, social activism at work, health and wellbeing, and hybrid work. I also describe challenges I have experienced dealing with these changes.

Diversity and inclusion intensify

At Xero I had a difficult learning experience about diversity and inclusion (D&I) beyond the traditional focus on gender equity. I was well grounded in the compelling rationale behind the benefits of enabling and encouraging D&I, including better access to talent, better relationships with customers, and helping underserved and underrepresented people in our community.

This experience at Xero helped me appreciate that fully embracing D&I requires that you see and feel the world through other people's eyes and experiences and to withhold your personal bias or judgement.

What happened?

It started with someone publishing a post on our all-employees Slack channel that they could not join in Pride Month celebrations on the grounds of their religious beliefs. That someone held such beliefs was not surprising, but including the words 'I believe homosexuality is a sin' in an all-employees post was a big problem.

I read the post and felt very uncomfortable with those words being expressed. They were hurtful and wrong. Something like this had never happened before, and until this incident Xero had never removed a staff member's post from our unmoderated and freely available internal communications channel.

My human resources and internal communications team worked hard to deal with the issue and craft our response, as demands for one grew quickly among members of our queer community and their allies.

The response

The response that went out by all-Xero Slack post that day missed the mark. It started by thanking the staff member for sharing their beliefs and followed on by making it clear that as a company, we believed that all Xero people had a right to their own beliefs, and that regardless of the views expressed we stood strongly with our queer community and their right to celebrate Pride Month.

The mistake we made was in not categorically denouncing the hurtful words expressed in the post. This led to further turmoil, and despite senior people, queer and not, insisting that the views of the individual did not represent Xero, many people were hurt and dissatisfied with the response and argued that it had caused more hurt than the original post.

The next morning, a little over 24 hours after the initial post, we decided to remove the original post and provide a further response that denounced the words expressed. We also acknowledged that our initial response was unsatisfactory.

The fallout

Even though our queer staff members knew the views expressed were not supported by Xero, the fact that they were not immediately denounced triggered fear among those who have experienced the pain and hurt of similar views and behaviours in other walks of life. It undermined their sense of feeling safe in their work environment.

We later learned that the eventual departure of the employee who expressed that controversial view caused pain for members of our work community with similar beliefs and they now also felt excluded because they didn't feel safe being open about their faith.

The question that arose: How do you make sure all members of your work community feel included and safe in the face of issues where some have very different beliefs, or where the company expresses a belief or view that isn't shared by all?

Principles going forward

We learned a lot from this experience, most particularly that we must respond with much more involvement of representatives of the affected members of our community so we understand the issue or hurt through their eyes. Our response would have been more effective if we had recruited the most impacted Xeros immediately in the response process. None of those initially involved were members of our queer community.

We also concluded that while we will allow anyone to express their views, it is their responsibility to do so without harming others. If harming others is a likely consequence, they should refrain. The post did not need to contain the six harmful words it did.

We should always support an individual's right to their beliefs over the opinion or beliefs of those who are observing or judging them. In this case, queer people's existence and right to be queer takes priority over the right to express opinions of them by a third party. The third party is still entitled to their beliefs; however, they need to be accountable for communicating those beliefs at the appropriate time and place and in the right manner.

At Xero, we said, we want to create a work environment where people can be their true and authentic self. This experience made me realise that this is an aspiration at the discretion of the individual. We all have experiences, conditioning and insecurities that define how comfortable we are to be our true and authentic self in various situations and environments. Our role as a company was to create an environment where it is as safe as possible to do that; the rest is up to our people as individuals, as we can't dictate how people feel.

Social activism at work

Inspired by the LGBTQI movement and outrage surrounding the murder of George Floyd by police in May 2020, people have increasingly expressed their support for specific social causes at work. This shift is evidenced by the formation of employee resource groups (ERGs) and similar forums.

At Xero, people formed employee-led ERGs around a variety of causes such as inequality, gender equity, sexual orientation and the environment to activate change. Social activism among our people extended to the strong views on how we responded as a company to issues of the day.

In this domain, we grappled with many issues and tragedies, such as the Christchurch mosque shootings by a white supremacist and the ramped-up incidence of floods, fires and other environmental disasters around the world.

Social activism at work is a good thing, an extension of the human element of building an inclusive and engaged workplace. However, there are potential drawbacks to be aware of that are not easy to manage.

The first is the process by which an organisation decides whether or not to take a position on an issue, and the consequences if that position does not represent the beliefs or views of all its people.

There's a lot to be said for good planning and communication of the areas of social concern where companies will play and where they won't. However, the process of deciding and communicating why, where and how an organisation weighs in on a social debate or issue is not always easy.

When an organisation supports a cause that some of its people do not, it is important to acknowledge and respect the contrary views and the rights of those who hold them to have those views.

For example, in the case of Roe vs Wade, at Xero we made it clear that we supported the rights of women to choose, rather than have lawmakers or other third parties exert their will over them. We also drew a line on the extent to which we played an activist role on the issue, rejecting the view of some of our people that we should not do business in US states that outlawed abortion.

The second area of concern with social activism at work is the potential distraction from the real reason we are there at work. In the case of Xero, this is to best serve our small business customers with great products.

It may be unpopular to say, but in a world of distraction and more distance between people at work than ever, it is important that we don't pursue social issues at the expense of the 'meat and potatoes' of why organisations exist. As the old saying goes, 'Nothing happens till someone sells something.'

Health and wellbeing go mainstream

The pandemic was a catalyst for bringing more attention to wellbeing in the workplace and the de-stigmatisation of mental health issues.

Health and wellbeing are closely related to work/life balance. I've always believed that work/life balance is about much more than the hours you work. It is defined by how you feel when you get home after a day's work. Do you feel good about what you accomplished and experienced or do you feel wrung out, exhausted and unable to engage fully with your family?

At Xero we did a lot of work to encourage the importance of wellbeing and mental health. In New Zealand our then Managing Director, Craig Hudson, funded access for all our accounting and bookkeeping partners to the support and assistance service provided to our Xero NZ employees. Craig has helped many people by openly sharing his own mental health challenges.

We hired Lucas Finch as our Global Head of Wellbeing to help make sure we had the right strategy and frameworks to encourage wellbeing at Xero. I came to better understand from the work Lucas and his team did that wellbeing at work touches on three distinct layers of focus:

1. **the individual** — doing what we can to help our people be more aware of and take personal ownership of investing in their wellbeing

2. **the company** — the programs, policies and practices available to support the individual wellbeing of our people

3. **the day-to-day experience at work** that we create for our people. Do they have clear objectives and the support needed to do their jobs well?

This third area resonated most for me, because it aligned attention on wellbeing at work with the quality of the day-to-day work experience of our people. Nothing impacts negatively more on wellbeing at work and work/life balance than a poor day-to-day work experience. This can be caused by poor leadership, unclear expectations or deadlines, indecision or inadequate resource allocation, and lack of prioritisation, to mention just a few.

Hybrid workplaces and finding the right balance

The pandemic changed the nature of workplaces. Almost overnight we were forced to operate remotely from our people and customers. Fortunately, Xero had the culture and technology to adapt quickly to these new conditions.

Trent Innes, Managing Director of Xero Australia at the time, was invited on industry panels to discuss the transition to fully remote work in the face of the pandemic. Trent had one significant observation that he shared with me after several of these events: 'Steve, many of these organisations just don't trust their employees.' At Xero, we benefited from the high trust between the company and our people, so the transition to remote work went smoothly.

Remote work was not new to me. In my five years as Xero CEO, I had no office. I worked from any available meeting room and, like anyone in the business, was asked to vacate the room if I hadn't booked adequate time and it was needed by others. More than half my time I travelled to other Xero offices around the world and worked from those offices, or in hotels or airplanes.

The initial approach at the height of the pandemic was clear. The health and safety of our people came first. Supporting our customers and partners facing difficulty followed quickly after. The message I gave our people was to 'just do your best'. None of us knew exactly what that was, or what lay ahead; however, I received a lot of positive feedback that people appreciated the message and the show of trust. We stepped up communication with weekly all-hands meetings, stayed close to our people managers and updated our people on the state of play as best we could.

We supported our customers and partners by providing help to navigate the various government subsidies and support mechanisms available, and building tools to streamline the administration of those subsidies under national digital initiatives, such as 'Single Touch Payroll' in Australia.

We replaced our in-person events, such as our company kick-off meetings and Xerocon, with virtual video events like 'Xero Online'. It was pretty remarkable how we and others adapted, testimony that necessity is truly the mother of invention.

As we moved past the worst of the pandemic to more normal operating conditions, the big issue that arose, and remains, is to define the best approach to this new 'hybrid' work environment.

For companies such as X (formerly Twitter), it was back to the office. For others, like Atlassian, it was to fully embrace remote work. There's no single approach that fits all companies. Ultimately it is for leadership to determine what best suits each organisation and team.

I have reservations about switching to fully remote work and believe that a solid base of in-office contact is important. The importance of in-person contact was reinforced when I bumped into a group of our fully remote employees in London, who said they most looked forward to their quarterly in-person visits to the Xero office. Fully remote work is here to stay and provides access to additional talent. The question is how prevalent it becomes in your hybrid work environment.

In-person contact is key to connection, not just with work colleagues, but also with the bigger-picture purpose and culture of the organisation. Hangout, Teams and Zoom meetings are great tools, and have their place, but they do not allow for the less structured interactions that can lead to 'accidental collisions' of ideas between people that inspire innovation.

At the time I retired as CEO of Xero I had not come to a clear view on the way forward. However, a number of principles had emerged that can shape effective hybrid work environments. These principles include the following:

- Hold regular all-hands meetings, hosted by senior leaders, where the broader company (and functional) purpose and strategy are communicated and reinforced.

- Expect people leaders to establish and account for a minimum amount of time that their teams and those they work closely with meet in person in the office. The nature of the work and geographic distribution should guide what is most appropriate. Also consider the person's role and the time they spend meeting and communicating with co-workers.

- At least twice a year, hold a meeting of all people leaders with the organisation leader to strengthen the direct connection between top management and those who lead the people in the business. Given the distractions and the distance between people in the post-pandemic world, this direct connection is more important than ever.

Making sure people leaders are close to their teams, and setting clear objectives and expectations, helps keep a focus on performance in a less physically connected working environment. The many distractions and increased physical distance between people will require management discipline to ensure organisations operate efficiently.

The eight Must-Dos that follow in Parts II and III provide a pathway to addressing these new workplace realities and the need to enable the full potential of people at work. But first, let's look at what drives people's resistance to change.

CHAPTER 3

CHANGE IS HARD BECAUSE WE ARE HUMAN

Our instinctive reaction in the face of change is one of fear, and for good reason. Our survival instinct conditions us to be wary of change until we fully understand its consequences.

If someone tells you there's an ambulance parked in front of your house, you assume the worst until you know your loved ones are safe. Fear is not a bad thing. If we were completely fearless, many of us would not be around today. Fear must be recognised and confronted as a force to deal with when we initiate or respond to change.

To fear change is human

In the work environment, we face many fears. Here are just a few of them:

- **Fear of not knowing the answer or of being wrong**. This fear limits what we ask, say and learn. In a changing world there's no such thing as a dumb question, so it's important to overcome this fear.

- **Fear of failure and making mistakes**. This fear limits what we try and what we learn. In changing times you can't separate making mistakes from learning, as long as the same mistakes are not repeated.

- **Fear of hurting someone's feelings or of not being liked.** This fear leads us to avoid having difficult conversations, giving honest feedback and making tough prioritisation decisions. As a result, we end up doing too much, lose focus and don't do anything well.

- **Fear of confronting uncomfortable realities.** Rather than embracing what we know may be happening, we hope things will just work out or play out on someone else's watch.

Addressing the impact of fear on people experiencing change takes time and focus, but is too often brushed over. The result is resistance to or derailing of the change program or initiative, and poor teamwork.

> *Recognising and mitigating fear, rather than consciously or unconsciously proliferating it, is a leadership imperative.*

Making the workplace a safe place where people can speak up, try new things and challenge the status quo accelerates change.

After a Microsoft Australia company meeting, during my time as Managing Director, I was sitting with four people in my office and asked them for feedback on my presentation at the company meeting just concluded. Their initial feedback was very positive. I decided to push harder for a critique of my content and for thoughts about what I could have done better. Still nothing but positive feedback. Determined to test their conviction, I said, 'Come on guys, are you really saying there was absolutely nothing I could have done better? Nothing? I really want to know.'

Finally, someone spoke up: 'Steve, when you were talking about one of the topics you forgot to cover a couple of things you could have.'

'Could have'? More accurately 'should have', as the omission was quite material.

I thanked the person who spoke up and said, 'I really appreciate that, and you're right, I should have covered that off.'

I then asked them all to speak up more quickly and feel comfortable that when I ask for feedback, I really mean it.

The interaction was typical of how fear of hierarchy is a challenge to free and open communication and feedback. Even though it was my content being critiqued rather than my delivery, people still found it difficult to give me honest feedback.

We all need to open the door to receiving tough feedback by leading people through the process. Airing examples of where you think you might be going wrong or could have done better will encourage others to speak up and share their honest opinions with you.

It's hard to learn from success

Bill Gates once said 'Success is a lousy teacher', and the road ahead would prove him right.

Ken Olsen, the founder of Digital Equipment Corporation (DEC), which dominated the mini computer era of the eighties and early nineties, said, 'There is no reason for any individual to have a computer in his home.' Is it any wonder that DEC was badly disrupted when the personal computer wave broke? As we all tend to do, Olsen valued knowledge from past experience too highly.

When the internet emerged as an ecommerce platform during the early 2000s, why didn't the big established retail department stores, with the advantage of their scale, crush the emerging players who started with nothing?

Here's IBM's Chairman Louis V Gerstner Jr (as reported in *ZDNet*), underestimating how Amazon might transform retail and internet sales back in 1999: 'Amazon.com is a very interesting retail concept but wait till you see what Wal-Mart is gearing up to do.'

Gerstner noted that the previous year IBM's internet sales had been five times greater than Amazon's. He boasted that IBM 'is already generating more revenue, and certainly more profit, than all of the top Internet companies combined'.

In 2024, Google Finance reported that Amazon enjoys a market capitalisation of US$1.89 trillion, dwarfing Walmart (US$540.7 billion) and Costco (US$370 billion).

The 'disrupters' started with nothing, so it's fair to identify the source of failure among the traditional players as the mindset of their leaders and their reluctance to embrace change. This resistance to change was largely a function of the 'problem of success' — that is, the danger of being trapped in the thinking that created past success and being averse to change.

Past success and knowledge are potential killers in a fast-changing world. We tend to lean heavily on what we know and what served us well in the past, deriving our self-esteem from our knowledge. Unmanaged and unconsciously, it becomes a limiting part of our mindset and partly explains why we are generally better talkers than listeners. The IT industry has a graveyard full of once great companies whose past success set them on a path to irrelevance.

I joined IBM's minicomputer division over four decades ago as a university graduate. Back then the new technology trend was putting computers into mid-sized companies for the first time. IBM recognised the need to establish a separate division to nurture this new line of business so it wouldn't get lost in the culture and past success of its mainframe or big computer business. The downside was that each customer would have two IBM sales teams serving it — for minicomputers (the General Systems Division) and for mainframe computers (the Data Processing Division).

As one of two IBM sales representatives responsible for servicing the shipping company Overseas Containers (OCAL), I wanted to explore collaboration with my counterpart in the mainframe division. So I picked up the phone to make contact. Someone who sat close to Graham, the mainframe sales executive I was trying to reach, answered. At the time, we had desk phones rather than mobiles, and it was good etiquette to pick up the phone and take a message for your teammate if they weren't there to answer the call.

The conversation went like this: 'Hi, Steve Vamos here from General Systems Division. I'd like to talk to Graham.'

'I'll see if I can get him for you, just a minute,' said the person answering.

Then, despite his covering the phone mouthpiece, I heard him say, 'It's Vamos from the toy factory on the phone for you. Do you want to talk to him?'

This introduction reflected the negative attitudes in the mainframe core business of IBM towards the new minicomputer wave. By the way, it would be remiss of me not to mention that those of us from the minicomputer division named our mainframe brothers the 'Dead Division'!

The 'big systems' mindset and culture at the top of IBM was exemplified by comments said to have been made by Jim Cannavino, then head of the Data Storage Division (DSD) of IBM, to a large gathering of IBMers: that if God believed in distributed computing, he would have put your brains in your fingertips.

Cannavino, later head of the IBM Personal Systems Division, gave Bill Gates and Microsoft the go-ahead to ship Windows as a competitor to IBM's OS/2 operating system, when Microsoft was still under contract to IBM. Mindsets at play in that outcome for sure!

IBM tried very hard but never fully embraced the evolution of smaller computers. It was ultimately no surprise that the personal computer business was sold by IBM to Chinese manufacturer Lenovo in 2005.

IBM did a lot of great things in the small computer space (including the golf ball typewriter, the original IBM PC and great minicomputers like the AS/400). At its core, however, the dominant mindset always favoured

IBM evolving, as it has today, as a large-enterprise, large-systems (and now services) company.

Similarly, Microsoft's initial failure to realise its potential on the Internet landscape was largely due to the deeply entrenched success of Windows and mindsets dominated by past success and knowledge. When the iPhone was announced in 2007, the then CEO of Microsoft, Steve Ballmer, famously said there was 'no chance' the iPhone would take market share.

Who could believe the iPhone would single-handedly propel Apple's market capitalisation above Microsoft's just three years later, in 2010? It was also ironic when you consider that a few years earlier Apple was struggling for survival only to be saved in part by founder Steve Jobs' securing investment and a strong declaration of support from Microsoft and Bill Gates.

Past success and knowledge can get in the way of change, because letting go of what we think made us successful and adopting new ideas and beliefs is not easy to do.

Our conditioning at work is not 'change friendly'

Change is hard because more than a century of industrialisation has encouraged conformist thinking in our work lives. Typically, we were hired to do what we were told, rather than be free to change things or to create the future. I'll never forget a boss of mine at Apple yelling at me, 'Steve, don't think, just do!' when I challenged the rationale for an organisational change he was implementing.

Baby boomers (like me) and Gen Xers were employed, promoted and expected to do what we were told, to be in control, to not make mistakes and to know the answer to questions we were asked.

These expectations do help keep things on track, keep the machine running, and make our bosses look good or stay out of trouble with their bosses. They are still appropriate today when applied to things we don't want to change. For example, we don't want people individually changing well-defined standards like those applied to occupational safety, accounting or medical procedures.

If I'm lined up for heart surgery tomorrow, I value a surgeon who is in control, doesn't make mistakes and knows what they're doing. But even that needs qualification, because there's always the potential impact of change through an unexpected event, where a fixed way of thinking can be dangerous. For example, if my heart surgery takes an unexpected turn and the operation isn't going well, I want a surgeon who is open-minded and willing to listen to or seek advice from those assisting in the operating theatre, rather than plough on without consulting others.

Conformist conditioning limits our willingness to challenge the way things are and to drive change. When people at work today hear the boss say, 'We need to be more collaborative, creative and innovative', many will shake their heads in frustration or confusion. They ask, 'Why, who with and what for?' And what happens if something goes wrong?

Organisation and team leaders must encourage their people to speak up and then really listen to what they have to say about what is going on around them. Too often they undercompensate for the fear and reverence that status plays in their organisation. If leaders truly want their people to embrace and lead change, they must visibly demonstrate 'servant leadership', with their every effort aimed at enabling their people to lead.

If they hope to overcome the obstacles of fear, the dangers of clinging to past success, knowledge and conditioning, people who lead organisations must appreciate that the more things change, the less what they *know* matters. They need to go out of their way to listen to their people and encourage them to challenge and question them.

Part I: Key messages and consequences

- People are the source and force of change, and technology is the enabler.
    - We need to place far more emphasis on the human and relationship elements of organisation and team performance. Always remember, people are our greatest asset.
    - Don't underestimate the potential of your people. Encourage and enable them to be the best they can be.
- People and technology continue to change the nature of work and workplaces.
    - Diversity and inclusion means seeing the world through others' eyes.
    - The best strategy to create wellbeing at work is to build the most effective and productive team and work environment.
    - Work extra hard to keep your people connected in a world of hybrid work.
- Change is hard because we are human.
    - Recognise and mitigate fear, rather than consciously or unconsciously proliferating it.
    - Encourage people to give you tough feedback by airing examples for them of where you think you could have done better.
    - Past success and knowledge can get in the way of change, because focusing on past success can make adopting new ideas and beliefs hard.
    - The more and the faster things change, the less what we already know matters.

The two domains and eight Must-Dos in *Through Shifts and Shocks* provide a pathway for leaders and their teams to address these realities and challenges and create stronger organisations, teams and change initiatives.

PART II

'BEING' AND WHY CHARACTER MATTERS

The more experience I've gained the more I've come to appreciate that being good at change demands knowing yourself and being conscious of how you project to those you lead or partner with on the journey.

	Must-Do actions
BEING *Character*	1. Apply the <u>right mindset</u>
	2. Be <u>self-aware</u>
	3. <u>Care about people</u>
DOING *Words and actions*	4. Seek <u>clarity</u>
	5. Drive <u>alignment</u>
	6. Focus on <u>performance</u>
	7. <u>Have difficult conversations</u>
	8. <u>Make hard choices</u>

In Part II we explore the domain of *Being* and the attributes of *character* that underpin people's capacity to adapt themselves, their organisation and their team in changing circumstances.

Character is defined by the *Oxford English Dictionary* as 'the mental and moral qualities which distinguish an individual'. These qualities shape our behaviour and are most evident to others through our words and actions and the emotions they convey.

> *Our character is deeply rooted in who we are as human beings, reflecting the nature, nurture and life experiences that shape us.*

A team also manifests character, as shown by how people engage with and perceive the individuals in that team collectively. No two teams (or leaders) are the same, because no two people are the same. The subject of character, and how we develop it, is far broader than I can cover in this book. For our purposes I will focus on the three vital elements of character that have been most evident to me in shaping the organisations, teams and change efforts I have led or been part of.

Character matters most because the absence of the attributes of the first three Must-Dos has a significant impact on the words and actions that flow to the people involved in a change program or process. The good news is that our character (and that of the team we work with) can be developed with experience and conscious effort. The bad news is that flawed character, and an unwillingness to evolve or change, has a very negative impact on all fronts of work and life.

The make-or-break attributes of Being and character, from my experience, are reflected in the following Must-Dos:

- Must-Do #1: Apply the right mindset.

- Must-Do #2: Be self-aware.

- Must-Do #3: Care about people.

These attributes of character have a huge influence on the people supporting a leader and the fate of their organisation or team. We explore each one in the following chapters but first, to make sure we are on the same page on Being and character, chapter 4 provides further insight into how character (reflecting nature, nurture and life experience) forms and plays out, using me as an example.

CHAPTER 4

HOW CHARACTER FORMS AND PLAYS OUT

As for all of us, my character was influenced by who I was born to, where I was born and the life experiences that continue to shape my character today.

My parents, Peter and Kathy Vamos, were Hungarian refugees who arrived in Australia in June 1957. I was born in December 1957, which means I was with them in utero on the boat that brought them to Australia.

My parents taught me the importance of respecting other people, regardless of their background and standing in our community. They gave me an incredible gift that too many sadly lack, which was to like myself as a human being and to be comfortable in my own skin, most of the time.

I'm grateful for having been born in Australia, thanks to Mum and Dad's courage and struggles. This email from Dad offered me a glimpse into his character and their story.

On 6th December 1956, the night European kids get their presents from St. Nicholas, we attempted to flee from Hungary for the second time. Why was this attempt successful? Only because of the help of organised people smugglers we had hooked up with.

We were asylum-seekers, two of us among 150 000 escapees, who, in a three-month period after October 1956, 'invaded' a country of 8 million people. Austria, a country that had regained full independence only 18 months before.

To help deal with such a mass intake Austrians got help from the international community — mainly through dozens of charity organisations. The Austrians in turn extended help to us very generously.

We were not locked up, were given free public transport, were housed and fed and were allowed to work (many did get jobs).

For an engaged couple — your Mum 18, me 20 — they even accepted the Hungarian definition of adulthood, set at 18 instead of the 21 years, they had as a prerequisite for adulthood.

Thus we could get married without parental consent and did so by the town clerk/celebrant of the city of Wels — on 15th December 1956. A familiar date as you were born exactly one year later.

Having handed our cash to the people smugglers, we had free housing and three meals a day and were given a very small amount of pocket money that lasted only hours.

So when walking out of the Town Hall I observed the town market and I realised we had no money to buy even a couple of oranges.

Yes, we did have thorough screening: a half hour police interview to formalise being granted asylum. We got an ID card in return for their filing our fingerprints.

Just after Xmas my parents joined us and they got the same treatment — and we got some cash to buy oranges. (In Hungary such luxuries were not available.)

Then came the waiting for acceptance to immigrate to Australia. Waiting in uncertainty is the worst enemy of the stateless, on par with hunger. I never forgot the feeling of it during those six months. (Just think about the asylum seekers detained, having to wait interminably in horrendous uncertainty. You can understand why I am so against the spineless fear mongering, forcing or enticing politicians to take despicable decisions.)

Our visa came through in April 1957 as we had to get a sponsor (we owed this to the Steads, your grandmother Margit's relatives), navigate through several medical exams, several interviews at the Australian consulate in Linz. (One time the queue took us to the head at 3:30pm. That was fine for still getting the interview over in time to catch the last train back to Wels. But instead of being called to the interview room, the reception window was shut: our introduction to the Australian practice of 'afternoon tea'. So we had to leave and return later.) Once all paperwork was in hand we had to wait again — for passage.

Your mum's parents, emigrating to Australia via a stay in Paris, came through Linz at the beginning of April. They stopped over and shouted us separate hotel rooms.

At the time we were in a camp where we were sharing a 12-bed room with several families. So the overnight stay in Linz was most welcome.

In mid-May we finally got passage: left Austria by train from Salzburg through Milan, the French Riviera to Marseille (non-stop, with us locked in). Finally we became boat people on May 28th boarding the US Navy's General Taylor, a troop carrier from WWII taken out of mothballs. The good news was it only took 26 days to get to Sydney through the reopened Suez Canal.

And the best news was that our final journey began with you already on the way...

My father was a huge influence on me as a person and as a professional. He worked at IBM for 38 years in a variety of sales and technical management roles. I was always interested in the competitive nature of the industry and saw through his experience the ups and downs of winning and losing large contracts. This led to another significant character-shaping experience — following Dad and joining IBM in 1979 as a university graduate.

At that time most major IT companies had graduate hiring programs and invested significantly to grow their own talent, given the limited availability of people with IT experience in the industry. I benefited greatly from IBM's commitment to the development of their people through the training and on-the-job opportunities it provided.

In my 14 years at IBM I worked in Sydney, Canberra, Melbourne, Perth and Tokyo, and had several different roles that allowed me to rise through the professional and management ranks over time. These roles included Marketing Support Administrator, Systems Engineer, Sales Representative, Sales Manager, Branch Manager and, my final role at IBM, General Manager of the Personal Computer Division. IBM invested in me and prepared me for what lay ahead in my career.

Understand how life experience shapes you

An example of how my father and IBM together contributed to my character development is evident in my approach to gender equity.

Diana Ryall, former Managing Director of Apple Australia, Tracey Fellows, former President of News Corp Global Digital Real Estate, Pip Marlow, former CEO of Salesforce ANZ, and Jane Huxley, CEO of Are Media, all publicly acknowledge my support of their career journeys. Recognition from these super-talented and hardworking executives is the best reward a former boss and mentor can get!

My perspective on gender was shaped by two significant events. First was the mistake my brother and I made when we were quite young when we told our sister she couldn't do what we were doing (playing a game in the backyard at home) because she was a girl. My father overheard the comment and seized us both by the collar and said, 'If you ever again dare tell her she can't do what you can do … I'll kill you!'

To say the least, we got the message, and from that point on I understood the concept of gender equity very clearly. A good role model can go a long way!

The second significant influence was my experience at IBM in the early 1990s, when the company decided to make serious moves to address the lack of women in senior roles.

In a meeting of 12 IBM regional general managers and branch managers (all men) with Terry Baker, the second most senior executive in the company at that time, gender equity was a focus.

Terry was a tall, commanding man who shared his opinions very directly. We were assembled around a U-shaped table when Terry joined us to talk about gender diversity. It was a short speech, culminating with the pledge, 'In 12 months' time, two of you will be women.'

This didn't go down well with some of the men around the table, and a few responded that day by adopting a female name as an email alias. IBM followed through with Terry's promise, though. (One of the women was rushed into the role and struggled; the other, a very talented executive, became frustrated by the lack of flexibility of her position and left the company to prioritise her family.)

This marked the beginning of a significant effort to change the mindsets and practices of IBM to better support, recognise and promote female talent. As part of that process, along with many others, I attended a course that exposed me to the notion of unconscious bias. While role-playing an interview with a female candidate, I asked her about her plans around starting a family. At that point, I was pulled up sharply by the facilitator and asked why the question was relevant.

This experience, 30 years ago now, helped me see how I was unconsciously making a judgement about the candidate that was not my place to make. Today we are aware that a woman's plans to have a family should not be of concern to a hiring manager.

That experience changed the way I thought and acted, as Tracey Fellows, who was seven months pregnant when I hired her into a big job at Microsoft Australia, will attest.

For reasons others can better explain, women tend to doubt themselves more than men do. In a 2022 *Harvard Business Review* article, 'How Confidence Is Weaponized Against Women', authors Darren T Baker and Juliet Bourke interviewed 30 male and 36 female senior leaders in the UK. They found, 'The vast majority of the women we interviewed (33 out of 36) raised confidence (or lack thereof) as a central factor obstructing their own and other women's career progression.'

It was a very different story with the 30 men interviewed, with no mention of confidence impacting their career trajectories. Six of the men mentioned confidence 'only in relation to women's careers and, in particular, women's perceived lack of confidence'.

In my coaching work I did an exercise with a start-up management team comprising three men and one woman, where I asked them to rate themselves and each other on five attributes of their work performance. The men overrated themselves on three of five attributes, underrated on one, and had a match between self and others' opinions on one of five. The woman underrated herself on three and matched with the view of others on the other two attributes.

There is a view that if someone is offered a job and they have six of 10 attributes needed, a man will talk to the six he has, whereas a woman will speak to the four she doesn't have.

The message for managers of women is the importance of expressing your belief in their potential openly and encouraging them not to sell themselves short. A senior female executive I spoke to about my experience also stressed the need for male managers of women to admit when they get things wrong. Her view was that males are socialised to be strong and right and find it hard to show vulnerability by admitting failure.

The point I want to make is that, as is true for all of us, my character as a leader developed through the life and work influences and experiences that have shaped me and continue to do so. Character is a complex domain that goes to the heart of who you are and how you came to be that person and continue to evolve. I encourage you to think deeply about this.

> *Spending time understanding how life experience has shaped your character is a valuable investment, as is knowing yourself and becoming more self-aware.*

Much has been made of the need for leaders to be 'authentic', a quality that is hard to define but obvious in how people experience you. I have heard executives say, 'I need to be authentic with you ...,' but genuine authenticity is unstated, self-evident, expressed through your words and actions.

Many great contributions have been made on how life experiences impact our thoughts, emotions and physical health. (*The Myth of Normal* by Gabor Maté is one book I highly recommend.) Given the uniquely personal nature of how our character is formed, being self-aware is incredibly important to anyone's leadership journey. Make sure to invest the time to explore it.

In the next three chapters I focus on attributes that reflect your character and have the most influence over leading people and organisations through change and uncertainty. From my experience, great leadership character is demonstrated by people who:

- apply the right mindset to enable change — in the face of change, a mindset that cares for, connects with and enables others, is willing to take risks and make mistakes, and values learning more than knowing

- are self-aware and think about how they think — able to observe themselves under pressure and seek feedback to understand others' perspectives and build shared belief

- care for people and talent — motivated to serve others and create a safe environment for others to speak their truth.

Before we dive into these attributes, let's be clear about what leadership is all about and why these attributes apply to all of us, whether we are CEOs, Board Directors or front-line professionals.

We can all be leaders of change

Leadership is inconsistently defined. It is *not* management. Both are important, but they are different and should not be confused.

Leaders make change happen. They question why and how you do what you do and look to change it for the better.

I don't like hearing people referred to as 'just a manager, not a leader'. It is wrong to talk about leadership in a way that demeans management. Management is about doing what you do and doing it well.

The leaders we admire are inseparable from the change journey they inspire. In the technology industry, leaders like Thomas Watson (IBM), Bill Gates (Microsoft) and Steve Jobs (Apple) are associated with the impact they have had on the world and the change they led.

Leaders see opportunities to do new and better things to improve results and outcomes for people, and make it happen. Management ensures the people and resources of an organisation execute its purpose and priorities. It includes organisational, functional and people management. Each strand of management requires the assignment of someone with appropriate skills and experience.

Leadership is different. It is an attribute anyone, anywhere in an organisation, can demonstrate, whether they are on the front line or a manager higher up the ranks. Anyone who sees an opportunity to do something better, and is able to work with those around them to make it happen, is a leader.

Leadership and good management are both vital to the journey of converting new ideas or ways of doing new things into reality. More than ever organisations need good leadership and strong management to sustain success.

In figure 4.1, the tip of the iceberg is *what* we do and is generally visible and known to all. It encompasses the industry domain of the organisation, its products and services, advertising and distribution functions. While *what* we do is generally similar to others in the same industry, there can be big differences in *how* and *why* we do what we do.

How we do things can be invisible — for example, the process we use to manage customer issues and communication. It can also be visible in attributes of our product or service.

The bottom of the iceberg represents *why* we do things. It's our purpose, and reflects the motivation for what we do and how we do it, which can vary between two organisations in the same industry.

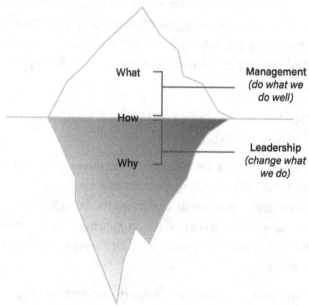

Figure 4.1: the iceberg — change happens below the surface

Leading change requires us to question how and why things are the way they are, and to challenge the current state of things.

The reason so many once-great companies fail is they end up doing the wrong things because their organisational leaders block real change to their collective why and how.

If you accept that constant change defines the conditions under which we operate, and that leadership is all about change and the human element, then you'll also recognise that leadership is the fundamental element of organisational survival and success, and that we can all be leaders if we really want to and are supported.

In the next chapter we look at the first Must-Do of Being and character: adopting the right mindset to enable change.

Key messages and consequences

Change is challenging for all of us in different ways and to different degrees, depending on our individual makeup and life experience. Understanding yourself, why you think the way you think and why certain things trigger you, is important to developing your ability to lead and respond to change, especially when facing into fear or under pressure:

- The character of leaders and teams is fundamental to the quality of teamwork and change.

- Understand how life experience has shaped you. Study, read and seek coaching, counsel and feedback to do the work on yourself, to explore the source of any insecurities you have that will trigger the wrong mindset and behaviour when confronted by stressful situations and change.

- Anyone can be a leader if they are motivated and focus on the *why* and *how* rather than just executing the *what*. Consider how much of your time each day is spent on the *why* and *how* you do what you do, rather than on *what* you do.

CHAPTER 5

MUST-DO #1: APPLY THE RIGHT MINDSET

The IT industry's graveyard is populated by once successful companies that failed because their leaders' mindsets were fixed on sustaining past success rather than embracing new trends.

Experiencing the turmoil at Apple during the mid 1990s, I came to understand the connection between the character of leadership and the fortunes of a company. During that time Apple went through three different CEOs — Michael Spindler, Gil Amelio and Steve Jobs — and it changed a lot, reflecting the different mindset of each leader.

Michael Spindler, who replaced John Sculley as Apple CEO in 1993, believed that Apple had to be more like Microsoft and Intel to win. Towards the end of Michael's reign, I was walking past his office at Apple's head office in Cupertino, California, when he called me in for a chat. Michael told me despondently, 'Microsoft and Intel have really fucked up this industry.'

I was stunned both by the statement and by the extent to which Microsoft and Intel were dominating Michael's thinking. His attempts to counter the dominance of the Wintel platform at the time led him to launch low-price (but high-cost) low-end Macs. This included a cloning program where third parties would be licensed to build and sell Mac-compatible products under their own brand, and Apple building products (displays and printers) that could operate in a Windows-dominated PC world.

The quality and differentiation of the core Mac proposition diminished because Apple was trying to do too many things. Spindler's low-end, low-price strategy contributed to massive inventory write-downs as sales stalled and confidence in Apple waned.

Gil Amelio, known as a 'turnaround guy' following his previous success at National Semiconductor, followed Michael Spindler as Apple CEO in 1996. I attended one of his first meetings with the top 150 executives of the company. Gil introduced us to his book writer sitting at the back of the room, and confidently explained that the book would be written about how he turned Apple around.

He did write his book, though perhaps not the book he had initially imagined. *On the Firing Line: My 500 Days at Apple* was published in 1998. Despite Gil's best intentions and well-documented struggles, it wasn't long before Steve Jobs was appointed interim CEO. For the third time in less than three years, Apple had a leader with a different mindset and way of thinking about what the company would be and do. Each leader's mindset had a defining effect on the company.

Reflecting on these experiences and examples of disruption at play, I have come to believe that the fate of organisations and teams is defined by how their leaders and people think and act in the face of change. The same applies to an individual, which is why I encourage you to think deeply about your own mindset and about how you think in the face of change.

Our work environment has changed dramatically and will change even faster in the future, so the ability to embrace and respond to change is critically important. This need to be good at change is common sense, right? But not often common practice. Why not? Because many leaders of organisations and teams were not developed to work in the fast-changing and disruptive environment we now experience. Like me, they are products of a past 'industrial age' when we attained positions of leadership by:

- being in control (or at least looking like it)

- not making mistakes (or hiding them well)

- knowing the answers to questions we were asked (or being able to shuffle our feet and question the question or avoid giving an answer).

We were mentored and promoted by bosses and organisations that evolved at a time when the world changed relatively slowly, and when people at the top of the hierarchy had all the knowledge and power. We gained recognition and self-esteem from the knowledge we had built up. We were hired to do what we were told. We were expected to be the 'arms and legs' rather than the 'heads and hearts' of the organisations we worked for.

Conditioning and experience shaped leaders (like me) across most areas of our economy and society to default to the mindset of a control-oriented, mistake-averse know-it-all!

Of course this characterisation is a generalisation, and there are exceptions, but it is close enough to the truth when reflecting on what was expected in the past. This default mindset made sense when change was relatively slow, and knowledge and power were concentrated at the top of organisations.

The good news is that this default mindset is still an effective and appropriate way of thinking when dealing with anything you don't want to change. Financial reporting and safety procedures are examples of processes where a consistent approach or standard is essential. In these scenarios we demand consistency and predictability. There is nothing wrong with the fixed/default mindset in this context, assuming there isn't an immediate need for change or the current system isn't broken.

However, disruptive and fast-changing times demand a different way of thinking, an open, change-oriented mindset that cedes 'control' in favour of 'caring' and 'connection'. In times of change, understanding and respecting the demands, expectations and experiences of those in our work and social networks is critical.

Figure 5.1 (overleaf) represents three important shifts in mindset from one that dominated in our industrial-age past to the connected and fast-changing world we now live and work in.

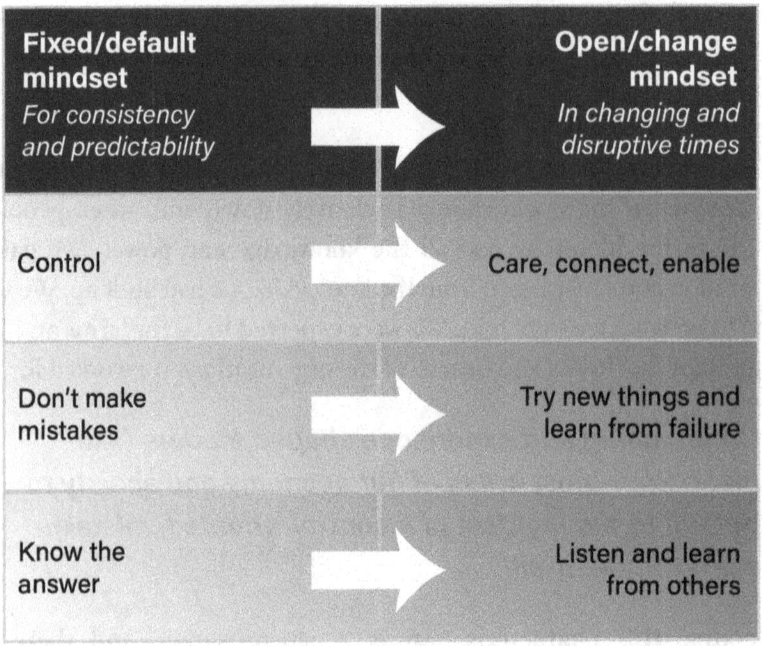

| Fixed/default mindset
For consistency and predictability | | Open/change mindset
In changing and disruptive times |
|---|---|---|
| Control | → | Care, connect, enable |
| Don't make mistakes | → | Try new things and learn from failure |
| Know the answer | → | Listen and learn from others |

Figure 5.1: apply the right mindset

In the face of change, we must:

- let go of our inner 'control freak' and direct our energies to helping and enabling others

- confront and help overcome fear of making mistakes, through a willingness to try new things and to fail on the way to learning and success

- let go of the know-it-all mindset expected by our predecessors, in favour of really listening to and learning from others, regardless of where they stand in the organisation or the social pecking order.

In a fast-changing world everything you know, or think you know, puts you at risk.

The need to embrace a mindset that is open to change is common sense and conceptually simple but hard to do in practice because it requires us to overcome our human fears, insecurities and past conditioning, and apply a high level of self-awareness.

When leading and responding to change we need to become far more conscious of our thinking and apply a mindset that is better suited to it.

Mindset shift 1: from control freak to connector and enabler

My experience as CEO of ninemsn profoundly changed my mindset. Founded in November 1997 as a joint venture (JV) between Kerry Packer's Publishing and Broadcasting Limited (PBL) and Bill Gates' Microsoft, ninemsn had resources that most start-up CEOs could only dream of.

The vision for ninemsn was to build an online presence for the group's magazine titles and Channel Nine television programs, and to provide the entry point for Microsoft's consumer online services into Australia, including Hotmail, Messenger and Search. I joined the business as CEO in March 1998.

The joint venture was born with plenty of money (with a commitment of $50 million funding from each partner), access to the best technology available at the time, and a bunch of smart people who were hired from leading media, technology and communications companies. An accomplished group of experienced industry executives had been assembled, their success reflected in the luxury cars parked behind our Paddington office.

Both JV parties assigned the online rights to pretty much all their respective businesses to the joint venture; ninemsn had everything (money, technology, smart people and highly recognisable media brands) that you could imagine and reasonably want in any online start-up at the time. What ninemsn did not have at its birth were the human and relationship bonds or structures of an established business.

The day I started my personal assistant Annette warned me that the place was in desperate need of adult supervision. One of the first staff issues I had to resolve was dealing with disappointment from several of our team members that we were not going to shut down the company for a few days for the annual Mardi Gras celebrations.

The company was just a few months old, had quickly hired about a hundred people, and had little or no structure or discipline. In 1998 there was no online media advertising industry, and no playbook for how to run an online media business.

For the first time in my career, I was leading a business that had no established culture or ways of doing things. To top it off, I had no knowledge or experience of the media and advertising industries. I was running a business in an industry I knew very little about.

In my first year as CEO I went to every meeting as the person who knew least about the subject matter being discussed. All I could do was shut up and listen, consider what I was hearing, then play back what I'd heard about the problems we were facing and suggest ways to overcome them. I also saw how the various players on the team behaved with each other, who was making a constructive contribution and who was getting in the way of progress.

Out of necessity and as a by-product of my limited domain expertise, I moved into the role of 'connector and enabler' of others. I became obsessed with ironing out the issues and misalignments that got in the way of people doing their best work.

The payback was immense.

There's a saying: 'The fish don't see the water in the tank.' The intangibles that bind organisations, the things you can't touch or see, tend to be taken for granted. At ninemsn, given my lack of domain expertise, all I could do was try to 'see the water' and make it cleaner and clearer for our people.

In early 2002, almost four years into the journey, we had survived the dotcom crash and emerged as the online media industry leader of the time.

Around that time, as I sat alone in my office leaning back in my chair and gazing at a blank wall, the realisation hit me that having little domain experience in media and advertising, the core of the ninemsn business, had been a blessing in disguise. The focus I had on helping others rather than exercising my individual skills had led to our creating a great team in a business that was growing fast and was loved by the people working in it.

For the first time in my career, I truly appreciated the importance of the human dimension of business and the value of intense focus on how people in an organisation work together.

Organisation leaders tend to overrate their knowledge and importance and underappreciate the critical role they play in enabling the success of others. They generally spend too much time doing what the business does, rather than immersing themselves in how it is done. As a result, the hard prioritisation and people misalignments that exist in organisations are not dealt with quickly enough, or at all.

My first three years at ninemsn were nothing but hard work, difficult conversations and hard choices. Changing times demand tremendous focus on connecting with, caring for and enabling people to embrace change, and committing to eliminate obstacles to their performance and success.

There could be no better illustration of the futility of a control mindset in times of change than the situation so many of us confronted with the initial impact of the COVID pandemic in early 2020. No one had any idea how things were going to pan out. My message to our people at Xero was simple: 'Do the best you can to keep things at work moving while at the same time looking after yourself and your family.'

I received a lot of positive feedback from people who were relieved to hear that message, because I handed them control over their situation, rather than pretending I could tell them what to do or control their approach to work. To all our communities, internal and external, the message was that we needed to stay connected, and share our experiences and learning, to get through the uncertainty and change confronting us.

Let's face it, it's impossible to control things when they are changing around you.

Mindset shift 2: from fear of mistakes to embracing the learning

A day in the life of a young child is one of experiencing failure after failure or mistake after mistake. Learning to sit, crawl, walk and talk is all about trial and error, mistakes leading to progress and doing new things, with constant encouragement and coaching from parents.

> *There's nothing, and I mean absolutely nothing, you are good at today that you didn't get good at by making mistake after mistake until you became good at it.*

Think about it. When leaders ask people around them to change things for the better or to be more creative, innovative and collaborative, they might as well say, 'Hey! Start making more mistakes!'

How leaders react to mistakes and failure is core to their character as leaders. Their reaction will directly affect the willingness of people to overcome their fear of making mistakes and to lead and embrace change.

'Fail fast, fail often' is business advice we hear a lot these days, but it takes more than simple one-liners to overcome the conditioning and hierarchy that breed fear of failure and making mistakes.

There are three things leaders need to do to enable their people and organisations to embrace mistakes and failure as learning.

1. Provide a clear context for mistake making and failure

This means going out of your way to explain:

- why change needs to happen

- what needs to change

- what success or a better outcome might look like

Being clear provides a safe space and context for people to do things in new and different ways rather than conforming to existing norms.

This context is important to ensure mistake making is not invited where change to the current approach or process is unwanted.

2. Encourage people to consider the worst thing that could happen and how that risk can be mitigated

When taking the risks associated with doing new things, consider the downside risk of what is being attempted and how the impact can be minimised or managed. While mistakes provide beneficial learning, this doesn't preclude the need to take care in areas that could have significant customer or stakeholder impact.

3. When mistakes happen, react supportively

I was an IBM Australia sales manager in our Canberra office, hoping to close a big deal with a university. I was fortunate to have then CEO of IBM Australia, Brian Finn, helping me and a senior account manager leading the sales process.

Brian repeatedly warned me that he thought we were going to lose the business, but rather than really listen and be concerned, I was confident, given the relationship my account manager had with the Vice Chancellor — they regularly drank sherry together.

As decision time approached, and following a further warning from Brian, I asked my account manager if there was any way the deal might fall through. He assured me that couldn't happen given his close relationship with the customer.

A few days later I noticed my account manager hadn't come into work at his usual time and wondered if he was okay. Later that morning he called me to let me know that the customer had decided to buy from another vendor. Our assumption that the customer would recognise value in the higher price of our offering was wrong. They chose the cheapest solution.

That news was bad enough, but even worse, I had to telephone Brian to let him know. I'll never forget how he responded when I told him we had lost the business.

Rather than being angry with me and saying, 'I told you so' (which would have been fair), he simply said, 'Steve, I'm really sorry to hear the news, but I hope this offers some clear learning for you for the future.'

I learned a lot from that experience (and lost a lot of sleep). Thereafter I rarely misread my chances of winning or losing a deal. I became a much tougher and more detailed qualifier of our chances. I learned and got better from making this mistake. The bigger lesson from Brian was the power of being calm and respectful towards those who try and fail.

> **How leaders respond to bad news and mistakes has a profound effect on the willingness of people to try new things.**

Mindset shift 3: from know-it-all to learn-it-all

Most of us derive self-esteem from showing others how much we know. The problem, at a time when things are changing so fast, is that what we know becomes less important every day. It is far more important to ask the right questions and to keep learning.

I loved the education sessions David Leckie, Nine Network CEO, gave me about the workings of the media industry when I was CEO of ninemsn. With my lack of previous media industry experience, I got great value from David's willingness to share his experience with me.

David spoke with clarity and certainty about the industry and business of mainstream media. He was also self-aware enough to tell me, only half seriously, 'Steve, I'm often wrong, but never in doubt!'

David showed great curiosity and interest in the development of the online business. Behind his larger-than-life persona, he was one of the best executives I met in the media industry. He knew when to listen and when he could rely on his own experience and knowledge, and he did so forcefully.

By contrast, another executive I worked with at IBM was a major know-it-all. I had the challenge of dealing with this executive to extract vital business administration and operations functions to support the spinoff of the IBM Personal Computer business from the mothership in the early nineties. He would bombard me with his knowledge on every subject and then some. I found meetings with him incredibly draining because he would not listen to what I was saying and would try to control me and the way I went about things. In frustration, I complained to another peer of mine.

'Dealing with this guy is driving me crazy! He's a complete know-it-all! I could ask him a question about nuclear physics and he'd know the answer.'

My colleague looked me in the eye and said, 'Steve, I hate to tell you, but he has a degree in nuclear physics!'

I couldn't win.

Knowing it all (and we all have that tendency from time to time) is dangerous because it stifles the change process, which is inherently about navigating the unknown. A know-it-all mindset is unsuited to changing times, when opinions should be recognised as just that. As Satya Nadella, CEO of Microsoft, said in a meeting with the Telstra Board (and also expressed in his book *Hit Refresh*), 'I'll take a learn-it-all over a know-it-all every day.'

Satya's open/change mindset has brought an important shift for Microsoft. The know-it-all gene has always been strong at Microsoft, originating from when Bill Gates led the company at the height of the Windows boom when fulfilling its vision of a computer on every desk. That mindset didn't translate well for Microsoft when the industry changed, and the Internet emerged as the platform for software as a service.

The search product group in Microsoft genuinely believed it could catch and outpace Google, when objective perspectives suggested otherwise. This same mindset led to the most popular free email service, Hotmail, being renamed 'Windows Live Mail', before being changed back to 'Windows Live Hotmail' after pressure from many inside the company who could not understand the decision to trash one of the world's top online media brands at the time.

The rationale for the change was obvious: to protect and build the Windows brand and franchise, which was the basis of Microsoft's success. But often what we hold on to that worked in the past may be irrelevant or damaging to the future.

As the world changes ever faster and more unpredictably, we must be more prepared than ever to let go of the knowledge that got us to where we are today.

Figure 5.2 is a picture worth keeping in mind. Nothing we know or do should be seen as 'sacred'.

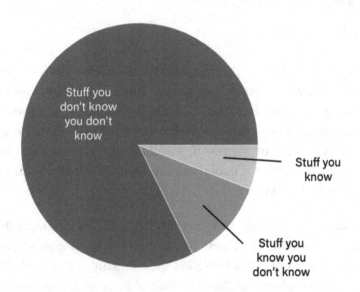

Figure 5.2: stuff you don't know

In considering our mindset, and the shift from a fixed/default to an open/change way of thinking, it is important to stress that, depending on the circumstances, both are relevant. The challenge we all face is to make sure we apply the right way of thinking to the situation we face.

We need to be self-aware and to think about how we think, which is the subject of the following chapter.

Chapter summary

The open/change mindset needed in situations of change is very different from the fixed/default mindset that comes with our survival instinct and ego. Applying the wrong mindset to a change situation can make us look like a control-oriented, fear-averse know-it-all.

Questions to ask yourself (or to ask others about you):

- Am I a control freak?
- Am I afraid to take risks and make mistakes?
- Am I a know-it-all?
- Am I captive to thinking that created past success?

Recommended actions:

- In change situations:
  - Let go of your inner control freak and direct your energy into connecting with and helping others.
  - Be willing to try new things and manage the risk of mistakes or failure.
  - Be a 'learn-it-all' and value less what you know and more what you learn from others, regardless of their place in the organisation.
- Be conscious of the mindset you apply to the situation you are in. More on this in Chapter 6.
- Print figure 5.1 and put it on your wall, and reflect through the day on what mindset you are applying.

CHAPTER 6

MUST-DO #2: BE SELF-AWARE

The 'fixed/default' way of thinking is important when we intend to execute a task or process repeatedly and flawlessly without changing it. The 'open/change' way of thinking is vital when we are confronted by or initiating change.

To apply the right mindset in a particular situation, we need to be aware of how we are thinking. This is hard to do when under pressure or facing into our fears, which naturally push us to revert to the fixed/default mindset.

In *Breaking the Habit of Being Yourself*, Dr Joe Dispenza points out that brain scans show we operate in a conscious state only 5 per cent of the time, and that 95 per cent of the time we operate from the subconscious. Dr Nicole LePera, in her book *How to Do the Work*, explains how the subconscious allows us to run on autopilot when doing routine things like having a shower, brushing our teeth and driving to work. 'Every moment of the day, this subconscious mind is shaping the way we see the world; it is the primary driver of most of our (often automatic) behaviours.'

You aren't defined by what you think, because what you think and believe can change. Your thinking is conditioned by influences, experiences and choices made on your life journey. You can change what you think and believe. We all do, which is why community attitudes evolve over time.

You are the consciousness behind the voice in your head that asks, *Why did I think like that?* or *Why did I do that?* or *What's he talking about?*

Your consciousness is what makes you human and enables you to consider situations and to change course. Being fully conscious in times of change, uncertainty and fear helps you apply the right mindset to the situation you confront.

Each of us, in our own way, can benefit from finding ways to slow things down, to be self-aware and conscious of our state of mind when confronted with changing circumstances.

One example of how this works for me is in overcoming my tendency to be a know-it-all and dismiss something new as stupid. I've often had that thought and later been proven wrong. So often, in fact, that nowadays the voice in my head is conscious of this and warns me, *Think again Steve. Take another look. You've been wrong so often when thinking like this.*

Another way of looking at consciousness is through the lens of 'mindfulness'.

It has taken time for me to overcome my resistance to the concepts of mindfulness and meditation. At my most ignorant state, I didn't see the need to meditate given I already get a solid eight hours of sleep a night. Fortunately, the voice in my head said, *Think again.* So I decided to learn about the practice of mindfulness. I now appreciate that these concepts are about slowing things down, being present, and being conscious in stressful and changing times. Breathing practices can also help us become more conscious and self-aware.

During COVID, in 2021, the members of my executive team were under significant stress from the pressure and physical disconnection caused by the pandemic, with restrictions on travel and being in the same room together. I found getting through a week of wall-to-wall video calls incredibly hard. I renamed Thursday, 'Friday eve', as a coping mechanism and reminder that the end of the week wasn't far away.

Doing yoga most mornings and getting in a 45- to 60-minute walk every day were hugely helpful. The atmosphere around my executive team was incredibly tense, though. I needed to find ways to improve our virtual time together. The catalyst for exploring something I naively thought was too obvious to be important and impactful was Cheryl, my partner.

Cheryl met Fraser Beck when she spent a week at the Aro Ha Wellness Retreat near Queenstown, New Zealand. At the time, Fraser was a senior retreat leader and breath coach at Aro Ha and the founder of a health education company, Optimal Health Model (Ohm). Cheryl found great benefit in the sessions with Fraser and thought they could potentially help my stressed-out team.

Fraser created short interventions during a three-day, virtual executive team offsite. While doing the breath work together felt weird at first, Fraser educated us on the benefits of each exercise, which helped us get over the awkwardness and embrace the learning. He helped us better understand how breathing is the epicentre of human function, with the power to correct our posture, focus our minds, balance our emotions and down-regulate our nervous systems.

I started to apply the 'box breathing' technique Fraser taught us when struggling to quiet my mind before sleep at night. It's a simple practice: five seconds breathing in — five-second pause — seven seconds breathing out — five-second pause; repeat the cycle four to five times. The next morning I'd wake up and find relief at how quickly I fell asleep after applying the technique.

James Nestor's book *Breath* reinforced the principles and insights Fraser shared and broadened my understanding of the nature and power of breath in helping address many of the stresses and associated ailments of modern life. I wish I had understood the connection we have with our breath decades sooner.

Whatever mindfulness technique you choose or develop is up to you, but make sure you find one! It will help you to discover ways to be more conscious of the mindset you apply in new and changing circumstances. An effective way to do this is to invite others to give you feedback on your behaviour and way of thinking, especially in situations in which you are under pressure and unconsciously applying the wrong way of thinking.

We're fortunate to have access to resources such as Nicole LePera's book *How to Do the Work*, which unpacks the possible impediments to our showing up to our full potential and provides a pathway to addressing them. Another great resource is *Clear Thinking* by Shane Parrish, which explains how we can be more conscious and react better in tense moments.

> *Being conscious and observing yourself opens the door to understanding yourself better and developing your character. Recognise what triggers you to respond in ways you wish you didn't and find ways to counter those impulses when they arise.*

Listen and seek feedback

In my early development as a people manager, I learned how feedback is a gift and a key to self-awareness. I benefited from the fact that IBM valued and developed people management as a specific skillset. Being a good people manager was treated as a top priority and responsibility, on a par with achieving great sales or meeting other business targets or objectives.

IBM people managers took a feedback survey at the six-month mark following their first appointment. At the time, as a new manager, I thought I was doing a great job. I was just the kind of manager I always wanted to work for. Or so I thought. The feedback from my direct reports told a different story.

The people who worked for me thought I was single minded and task oriented and had no real time or concern for them. That shocked me! I learned that how I saw myself as a manager could be quite different from the experience of people who worked with me. The feedback led me to think differently and change how I managed people. It also led me to seek feedback from my people outside of the formal processes and encourage them to speak up and give me 'therapy' if they thought it necessary.

I learned more from feedback than from any formal management course I ever attended. The lack of regular, open and honest feedback on the performance of people managers is a big impediment to their development. And it is a big part of why, when it comes to the quality of people management and the environments they create, 'common sense is often not common practice'.

IBM instilled the importance of great people management as a top priority for me, and I carried that experience on to Apple, ninemsn, Microsoft and Xero.

People leaders are the vital link between the aspirations of an organisation and the day-to-day reality for people at work. Turning strategy into action depends on having good, well-aligned people leaders in the team and throughout the organisation. For these reasons, it is super important to understand the quality and experience of people leaders in the organisation and their respective employee satisfaction, surveyed through whatever system makes sense for your organisation.

Removing consistently poor people managers from that role will improve performance and support good execution across the business. Making sure there is consistent feedback on the executive team and management must be top priority for the organisation leader. Poor performance by senior executives or senior managers has a much bigger impact on the organisation than poor performance by an individual team member because of the influence they have on setting objectives, allocating resources and making important trade-offs.

If you are serious about developing your character and those of other leaders, make sure to genuinely seek feedback from the people you work with.

One approach to seeking feedback that I find helpful is 'do more/do less' facilitated feedback. As a team leader I have subjected myself to this process several times. It can be uncomfortable, but it works.

First, find a facilitator you and your team trust. Put your team and the facilitator in a room together, allocating two to three hours for the session. Next, after expressing your genuine desire to hear their truth and learn how you can be better, leave the room and have the facilitator discuss with members of your team:

1. what they appreciate most about you
2. things they want to see you do more
3. things they want to see you do less.

After they have completed their discussion and taken a short break, re-enter the room for the debrief by the facilitator with the team present. Then have a constructive discussion of the feedback, with an opportunity for the team leader to question and discuss. Remember, feedback is never wrong. Feedback is a gift without which improvement is hard. The process always opened my eyes to things I didn't see.

At a Xero leadership team meeting on Waiheke Island, near Auckland, I ran a do more/do less feedback session and learned that one individual on my team felt I treated them more harshly than others, and others on the team agreed. The crazy thing was that the person concerned was the one I had the closest relationship with and therefore, unconsciously, was more direct and demanding with. I realised from the feedback that my behaviour wasn't right and I became more conscious of that behaviour if it surfaced when I was under stress.

Being a great listener is an important enabler of self-awareness and a very tangible way of showing people you care.

A yes to someone's suggestion is a great endorsement, as can be a well-explained no or 'not yet'.

I was running the Microsoft Online Services group international business and US sales, and had the opportunity to occasionally meet with Steve Ballmer, then CEO, about the things we needed to do to improve our performance in the digital media space. I nutted it down to five things, which we debated. I was keen to see all five done. Steve, however, was convinced on only three of them. Even though I didn't get my way, I appreciated and respected his willingness to listen to me and explain why he had a different opinion.

It's kind of crazy, given how important being a good listener and regularly seeking feedback is, that most of us aren't taught the discipline of effective listening on our school and professional journey.

In his book *How to Listen*, author Oscar Trimboli distils what he's learned from conversations with hundreds of people in critical listening roles, including airport traffic controllers, hostage negotiators and judges, to understand the characteristics of world-class listeners. Taking time to learn how to listen better is a great investment to make.

Being a good listener enhances our professional reputation, personal relationships and leadership character.

Get a coach

At Xero I often shared by observation with accounting partners that running a small business is a complex human pursuit, yet businesses owners get less coaching than their children playing weekend sport or learning a musical instrument. I spoke about the need for accountants to pursue the opportunity to coach their client's small business as an extension of the accounting practice and services they offered.

In the following chapter I talk about how a team or organisation leader needs to act more as the head coach of their organisation/team than as the star player, and I do believe that. The reality, however, is that team leaders can't coach themselves the way an objective third party can.

The teams I led at Microsoft Australia and Xero benefited a great deal from having a coach observe our meetings and provide an objective source of advice and insight to me, as team leader, and to the individual members of the team. Sometimes I didn't like what I was hearing from that coach about their observations of my performance, but I always valued the opportunity to improve by acting on that feedback regarding dynamics I was oblivious to.

My brother, John, has made a career out of coaching and speaks better than anyone I know about why we benefit from objective third-party facilitation of business meetings and processes. He has written several books on the topic — most recently, *Four Voices*. John chairs and advises several significant family-owned enterprises that he helps make better decisions, lead and respond to change over time. Based on his research and practical experience, John believes that coaching is the non-negotiable X-factor in getting the best out of an individual and team.

I see a big future in the coaching space for small businesses and leaders of teams in enterprises as technology provides tools and capacity for accountants and others with the appropriate skills and experience to make this service much more economically viable than it has been to date.

The character domain is one where an external coach can make a huge difference. It's hard for a leader to lead their team and at the same time do the work to ensure the team functions as well as it can.

In high-performance or elite areas of human endeavour, coaching of individuals and teams is a serious and recognised function. In the even more complex domain of business, it's not so common.

At Xero, and in other roles, I found the engagement of a team coach to support me and the leadership team was super helpful and a great investment.

Belief is everything

It may be considered a cliché when sports stars ascribe their success to their belief in themselves, yet nothing could be truer. Your beliefs define you and your actions. A five-dollar note is worth five dollars because we believe in the connection between that note and the value of goods and services it can be exchanged for.

At the dawn of the online media industry in the late 1990s, the established leaders in the media industry believed that online ads would never pay and banners wouldn't work. This strong belief by those who knew most in the industry made no sense to me as a media industry novice, or as the CEO of an online media start-up. If a TV, newspaper or magazine ad paid off, why wouldn't the same apply to a computer screen?

I chose to believe that online media would pay. Fortunately for me, history proved the experts wrong. For the 2023 calendar year the Australian online advertising market reached $14.7 billion. It has delivered double-digit revenue growth in most years since the industry began reporting in 2002.

In 2000 digital advertising in Australia represented a 1 per cent share of total advertising revenue; in 2023 it stood at a staggering 67 per cent (see figure 6.1). Even more amusing to me is that the banners that were 'never going to work' do so well; TV screens today are plastered with them.

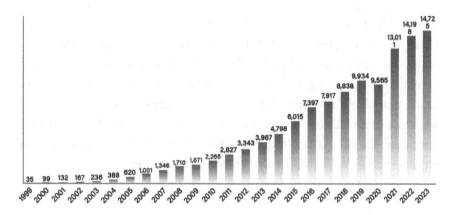

Figure 6.1: digital advertising in Australia, 1999–2023

Source: IAB Australia/PwC Online Advertising Expenditure Report

Working with start-ups has helped me appreciate how much belief matters. When I recorded a podcast with Xero founder Rod Drury, discussing his journey as an entrepreneur, his most striking comment was how he always had complete belief in his ideas and pursued them with a confidence that came from within.

There is no business without a founder who strongly believes in an opportunity.

There is no funding without investors who believe in a founder.

There is no new product without the cash from investors and their belief.

There is no revenue from customers without belief in the product.

We are what we believe, and in changing times we need to be extremely conscious of our beliefs and be prepared to suspend and change them if they are misaligned with what is going on around us.

When the dotcom crash happened in 2000, belief in the potential of digital media took a huge hit. Many sceptics celebrated, for a short time, what looked like a very big setback for the nascent digital media industry.

At the time I used the graph in figure 6.2 to show my team at ninemsn what was really going on. While the stock market had crashed, and many dotcom businesses folded, internet usage was booming and our revenue kept growing. I continued to believe, based on the underlying fundamentals of revenue and user growth (capturing 'eyeballs'), that we had a great value proposition and that one day digital media would dominate the media landscape. Figure 6.2 shows the fundamentals of our revenue growth and the ups and downs of the share market.

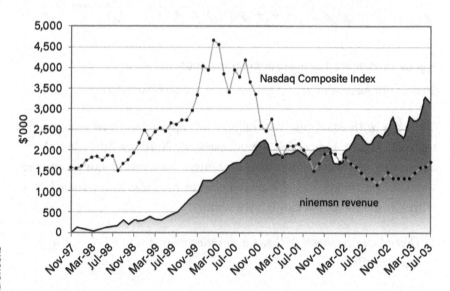

Figure 6.2: the dotcom crash

Henry Ford famously said, 'Whether you think you can, or you think you can't, you're right.' Never underestimate the power of belief and the need to share and build belief as part of any change journey.

Don't be a victim

One of the most limiting mindset traps is to think of yourself as a victim in the face of change. The 'victim virus' is not uncommon. You often hear it in the language of people you work with or do business with. Typically, it shows up in situations of difficulty and frustration.

At Microsoft, when I joined as Managing Director of Australia and New Zealand, the victim virus was evident whenever I'd ask if we could change or implement something new or different. The response would be 'It's a great idea but Corp (our US head office) won't let you do it.' There was some talk that I might be the shortest serving Managing Director in the subsidiary's history if I pursued my non-conformist ideas (the previous record was seven weeks).

Fortunately, I was recruited as part of a change mandate supported by executives above me who accepted that Microsoft needed to change. The executive behind the change mandate was the engaging Orlando Ayala, who served for many years as the leader of the company's subsidiary operations.

Another symptom of victim virus is when people refer to the company they work for in the third person. Brett Chenoweth, an accomplished executive, Board Director and friend of mine, was trying to establish a partnership for his start-up business with Australian telco giant Telstra. Brett kept hitting roadblocks with the executive who was key to getting arrangements in place. The process was dragging on and Brett was very frustrated by the attitude of the Telstra executive he was dealing with, who said, 'Really sorry this is dragging on, but you know what Telstra is like.'

Brett lost his cool when he heard this and said, 'No mate I don't know what it's like, and it isn't Telstra, it's you! You are Telstra!'

There are few things worse than hearing someone from a company speak like a victim of that company's management or inability to get things done.

Addressing the behaviours of victimhood is an important aspect of proliferating mindsets for change. The first step is to recognise the language and behaviour of victims. At Microsoft we ran a 'Victim–Leader' training exercise across the business with the help of an external consultant, Patrick Campiani. The training helped make people more conscious of what victimhood sounded like and how victim-like questions and responses can be replaced by responses that lead to a more constructive reaction to difficult situations. We encouraged people to be 'response-able', to be mindful of how they responded to difficult circumstances and whether that response was one of a leader or a victim — even though they might not be responsible for the issue or problem at hand.

The language of the *victim* inspires a conversation that asks:

- What happened to you?

- Who's to blame for what happened to you?

- Why do you think they did it to you?

- What should they have done instead of what they did?

- What should they do now to repair the damage?

- What punishment do they deserve for doing it?

By contrast, the language of a *leader* inspires a very different approach to the same situation:

- What challenge did you face?

- What response did you choose?

- Could you have responded more effectively?

- Could you have prepared better to mitigate the risks?

- Is there something you can do now to improve the situation?

- What can you learn from this?

An everyday example of the language of a 'victim' might sound like this:

'Sorry I'm late, the traffic was terrible. The council needs to fix the roads or they'll be voted out of office at the next election!'

The leader takes response-ability:

'Sorry I'm late, the traffic was terrible. I should have left home earlier given the roads need a lot of work.'

> *It's a natural human reaction to feel like a victim when change is thrust upon us. A test of character is how quickly you move through the victim stage to the mindset of a leader, who considers the situation and embraces the opportunity to respond (response-ability).*

Being self-aware and *thinking about how you think* is vital to being your best in situations of change.

Chapter summary

- Listen up! You have two ears and one mouth for a reason.
- You are not what you think or believe; you can manage or change it.
- Don't be a victim, be response-able.

Questions to ask yourself (or to ask others about you):

- Am I self-aware and fully conscious of my behaviour?
- Am I a good listener, regularly seeking others' feedback?
- Do I demonstrate and share belief in what we are trying to accomplish?

(continued)

- Do I move quickly from victim to leader when confronted by adverse situations?

Recommended actions:

- Develop your own rules, prompts and tools to help you pause in the moment between an emotion and a reaction. For example, be mindful by observing yourself as you would an actor in a movie or play, or by taking a breath before you react and speak, or by committing yourself to rules, such as never thinking something is stupid till you fully understand it.

- Feeling frustrated in the face of change is a natural human reaction, so recognise a victim state of mind and quickly transition to a 'response-able' leader mindset.

- Be aware of your beliefs in changing times and be prepared to suspend or change them if they are misaligned with what is going on around you.

- Get a coach for your team who can observe how you are working together and facilitate conversations on how that can improve.

- Proactively seek feedback that can help you develop and improve. For example, ask, 'What did I miss or what could I do better?' and then add, 'What else?'

- Use the do more/do less feedback exercise.

Refer to the Must-Do Toolbox:

- Practise feedback speed dating.

CHAPTER 7

MUST-DO #3: CARE ABOUT PEOPLE

In this chapter, we consider the Being and Character attributes that are key to demonstrating you care about people and talent. *If you want people to think you care, you have to care.*

Pause for a moment to reflect on these words and how they relate to the way we treat people who encounter us. Showing you care by listening to, helping and encouraging others is a foundation of great change, teamwork and life. It's a space where all of us can show leadership in whatever role we play.

Organisation and people leaders should care about the development of people. This is the focus of this chapter. For those not in leadership roles, this chapter outlines what good leadership and a great work environment look like and outlines positive attributes you can develop as an individual contributor.

Serve others before self

The motivation that drives anyone to take on a leadership role is a defining aspect of character. In his book *The Motive*, Patrick Lencioni helps organisation and team leaders reflect on *why* they are leading in the first place, and how that motivation drives their behaviour and willingness to take on the challenging work involved in guiding people and teams through change.

Through two fictional CEOs, Lencioni explores the motivations of *self* and *service*. The idea of 'servant leadership', modelled by one of his CEOs, has been written about and well documented. The other CEO has a highly self-centred leadership style oriented towards looking good and being rewarded.

I know which CEO I'd prefer to work with.

Another fascinating fictional study of this dimension of character is by the writer Robert Harris, in his novel *Conclave*, about the candidates running to be the next Pope. The least self-centric person in the race ultimately wins the race.

It is impossible for any leader to be solely of 'service' orientation. How we show up reflects the circumstances we face, such as the extent to which we feel secure in our role. Fear and insecurity can push us towards self-centredness. The source of that fear or insecurity can be extrinsic, generated by factors in our work environment. It can also be intrinsic and more hidden, originating from past experiences or childhood.

Leaders and team members I have worked with cover the spectrum. Some were transparently self-centred while others were selflessly dedicated to the service of others.

Many of my people management challenges as a Board Director and a CEO involved working with and helping people in leadership roles who were too self-centred.

Intrinsic self-centredness is hard to deal with because you really need to get inside the mind of the person concerned. Self-centred people are often super talented: they mean well but become their own worst enemies.

Having people around you who are willing to make personal sacrifices for the good of the business or team makes the change process much easier.

In Xero's FY21, which saw the onset of the global pandemic, we adjusted our budgets several times during the year in response to the uncertainty we faced. Each member of our leadership team had to contribute to expenditure cuts we needed to make. Some areas were hit harder than others, and while there was plenty of debate and discomfort around the approach we adopted, all members of the team bought into the process unselfishly because they were motivated to put Xero first.

Leadership character in the face of change, broadly speaking, is much better when those involved are service oriented and prioritise what is best for the organisation or team, rather than in their own interest. People who are willing to sacrifice their function or domain to help the broader team are the ones I want around me.

Create a safe environment for people to speak their truth

If you want people to contribute their best, you have to work hard to make it safe for them to speak up.

Research for Google's Project Aristotle sought to identify the factors that made for great teamwork. After two years of work that included over 200 interviews with Google people and considered more than 250 attributes of over 180 active Google teams, they identified a number of common characteristics of great teams.

They discovered that who was on a team mattered less than how the team members interacted, structured their work and viewed their contributions. The five key dynamics that set successful teams apart from other teams at Google were:

1. **Psychological safety**. Can we take risks on this team without feeling insecure or embarrassed?

2. **Dependability**. Can we count on each other to complete high-quality work on time?

3. **Structure and clarity**. Are goals, roles and execution plans on our team clear?

4. **Meaning of work**. Are we working on something that is personally important for each of us?

5. **Impact of work**. Do we believe fundamentally that the work we're doing matters?

Psychological safety was identified as the most important of the five dynamics. It underpinned the other four dynamics because it enabled an environment where people had the courage to overcome their fear of how other team members perceived their competence, awareness and positivity.

The safer team members feel with one another, the more likely they are to admit mistakes (which are inevitable with any change), to partner and to take on new roles. Individuals on teams with higher psychological safety were found to be less likely to leave Google and more likely to harness the power of diverse ideas from their teammates. These teams also brought in more revenue and were rated as effective twice as often by executives.

The need to make it safe to challenge one another cannot be overemphasised because it's a game changer. Keep in mind that a false form of psychological safety can be found in environments or cultures where people are unaccustomed to being challenged by those they work with.

At Xero we were conscious that our #human value and care for others was much more dominant than our #challenge value. People were reluctant to speak up and challenge or provide corrective feedback because they didn't want to hurt others' feelings. This condition is common to many work environments and won't fix itself without intervention.

To address the issue, we featured Kim Scott, the author of *Radical Candor*, at our Xero company kick-off meeting and people leader meetings. We also ran a training program on holding 'Crucial Conversations' to build this critical capability. Real progress here requires ongoing investment in training and strong modelling by people leaders.

Great character is reflected in the extent to which fearless, difficult conversations and healthy disagreements happen in an open and respectful way.

Value the strategic role of the HR function

I often ask CEOs and leaders of organisations if they have a strong Human Resources lead. Too often the answer is no. Having a great head of HR is like having additional CEO capacity to lead an organisation. I've learned to make it a priority, which has consistently benefited the change efforts and teamwork in organisations I've led.

I've been fortunate to work with great HR executives such as Maree Taylor, who worked with me as Head of HR at Apple Australia and Asia Pacific during the crazy times when things went from bad to worse. Maree coached me on how to link strategy to individual people objectives at a time of great uncertainty. This process gave our people confidence that we had a way forward through our challenges, and it has continued to serve me well.

The Human Resources function is often undervalued and underleveraged. Leaders of organisations with 50 or more people who don't have access to a capable HR Manager or a person with those skills are missing out.

As venture capitalist Marc Andreesen says 'If you don't start layering in HR once you've passed 50 people on your way to 150, something is going to go badly wrong'.

A strong leadership team is the primary team

Executing strategy and change demands people working well together across traditional functional areas and responsibilities. For this reason, having a great team at the top and across an organisation is more important than ever. Team members need to commit to the team they serve on as their 'primary team', ahead of the function they directly represent.

Too often leadership teams are not as effective or well aligned as they need to be. They can resemble a 'United Nations of Functional States' that meets to share updates and discuss areas of common interest without effectively tackling the big cross-business issues. Before I go too far down this track, I need to clarify what I mean by a leadership team.

A leadership team is a group of people with a *common purpose and interdependent goals*. If there is little or no interdependence, then they may not be a team, and it makes sense to question if they need to be brought together at all. It is important to ask: Is this team really a team?

> **Great teams have two attributes. All team members understand their interdependence and responsibilities to each other. And all team members treat their peers as their 'primary team', above the function they lead and the team that reports directly to them.**

Too many leadership teams of organisations see their individual functional or divisional teams as their primary team, rather than the team they participate in with their peers. The higher levels of collaboration needed to execute strategic initiatives across functions and divisions does not happen unless the top team is aligned and genuinely works towards a common set of priorities and actions.

My first leadership team meeting as Vice President, Sales and Operations, of Microsoft's Online Services group brought together 12 senior executives from around the world to discuss the state of our business and our forward plans. We met at a downtown Seattle hotel on the waterfront called The Edgewater, famous for floor-to-ceiling views across Puget Sound, and for a visit by The Beatles in 1964.

The mood in the room on arrival wasn't great. Traditionally these meetings didn't deliver much value. Everyone preferred to be at home doing their day job, rather than attending this meeting. Laptop computers were open and people were already buried in their daily hundred emails. As with other teams I'd inherited, they were a 'United Nations' of functional leaders who represented their individual interests and not the collective. I started the meeting with a scene-setting statement:

'You probably think the next two days are going to be a waste of time. You're all busy and would prefer to be at home just getting on with it. Am I right?'

No one responded directly, but the attendees' body language signalled that I was on the right track. I continued by asking them to consider how many people worked across our organisation in total.

'About 1200 people, right?'

They agreed.

'So here's the plan. We're going to delegate everything we do to the 1188 people not here today to give us more free time and take the pressure off. Do you think they'll notice the extra workload?'

The point I was trying to make was that our individual hours on the job and impact at the front line were negligible in the scheme of things.

I continued, albeit a bit tongue in cheek: 'Now our diaries are clear, we're going to spend all our time doing everything we can to enable those 1188 people to be successful, to work incredibly well together and to do the best work they can. We need to make sure they understand where we're heading — our priorities and expectations — and then do everything we can to address any lack of clarity or obstacles that get in their way. Get it?'

They did, sort of.

The point of our first two-day off-site meeting was to begin developing the clarity and alignment we needed as a team and accelerate our individual transition from 'doers' to 'enablers'. It took time, but over the next six months we did the hard work and planning needed to create a common agenda along with common goals and priorities that would be cascaded to all our people around the world. We also established a process by which we could measure and monitor progress.

Over time these meetings became something we looked forward to, with an agenda that engaged all of us because it was shaped by our areas of common interest.

If team meetings are boring, then you have the wrong agenda.

If an organisation has any hope of being well aligned and executing effectively, the top team must spend a lot of time together working on common priorities, issues and actions.

I was interested to read in Walter Isaacson's biography *Steve Jobs* that Steve and his team met every Monday morning for three to four hours. In Satya Nadella's book *Hit Refresh*, he talks about how the Microsoft leadership team meets for six hours every Friday. At Xero, the executive team I led met for at least four to six hours a week to discuss our business performance and execution of our strategy. This commitment of time was needed to drive our common agenda and track execution of important cross-business strategies.

Organisations that are executing poorly or below their potential will continue to do so until the right meetings are held to make sure priorities are clear and any issues are ironed out.

> *There are three kinds of meetings: good (fun) meetings, bad (waste of time) meetings, and hard, meaningful meetings where tough issues are discussed and resolved.*

Hard meetings involve difficult conversations and hard choices about issues that block strong alignment and progress. We had more than a few of these at Xero over the five years I was CEO. Hard meetings are most important because *they are the oil of change and progress.*

Be head coach more than star player

Many of us are promoted to positions of people leadership because we are experts of our function or domain. We were the star players in our position. As people leaders, we can't resist getting on the playing field to demonstrate our skills to those who work for us. We overrate the value of our domain knowledge and skills and tend to underappreciate the critical role we play in others' success. We avoid making the hard prioritisation choices and having the difficult conversations about performance and people misalignments in our teams.

If you have had the opportunity to perform a people leadership role when you did not have domain experience and weren't a star player, you learn more quickly what it means to become the head coach of your team. Seize this opportunity in your career journey if you can.

As mentioned earlier, for me that opportunity was my experience as CEO of ninemsn. I learned that a team leader needs to think like a 'head coach' rather than a 'star player'. I learned that I could deliver a lot more value to the organisation and team I led by clarifying team priorities and driving alignment of our resources with our objectives, rather than trying to be another expert on the advertising industry.

Having the domain skills and experience of a star player is a good thing, because people leaders need to step onto the playing field from time to time. Just be sure to prioritise your time on enabling your people to do the most important work and to be as productive as possible. Always look to recognise the potential of people and the team around you, and commit to clearing obstacles to their performance.

I love the expression we used at Microsoft: that a manager's role was to 'help make others great'. Are you a head coach or a star player? Find out what the people you lead or work with think.

Develop great people managers

If you (or a people leader who reports to you) don't like managing people, and are not inclined to get good at it, I recommend you get out of it (or I hope you or they are taken out of it).

Why do I take such a hard line? Because people who work for poor people managers deserve better. The people management function is aimed at bringing out the best in people and making sure they are contributing to their potential.

For the most part, people aren't looking for their manager to be a close friend. They are looking for a boss who cares about them and helps them get the job done. You don't have to be particularly nice to be a good people manager, though it helps. Good people management isn't babysitting; it's creating an effective link between the organisation's strategic intent and what people and the teams they work on do day to day in their jobs.

It's a mistake that so many organisations don't make good people leadership a priority for their people managers. As a result, most don't invest enough effort in building people leadership and management capability across their organisation. This neglect stems from overrating the individual contribution of people managers and underappreciating the important role they play in enabling the success of others.

I often ask business or organisational leaders, 'Are people management responsibilities the number one priority of all the people managers in your organisation?'

The answer is most often an uncomfortable 'no'.

To be even more explicit, I ask these questions: 'Are managers who consistently underperform in the function of managing people ultimately relieved of these responsibilities?' And, 'Is the feedback of employees about the capability of their manager gathered by survey or other means on an annual basis and used in the manager's performance assessment?'

The answers to these questions are also often 'no' and 'no'.

When I posed these questions in a conversation with a leader of a major IT company who was concerned about the low levels of staff engagement in his business, he responded, 'We have too many other things going on to load this on to what our managers are dealing with right now.'

I asked similar questions of the CEO of a major media company and his answer was, 'No, but every month I sit down and talk to a few staff members to find out what they're feeling.'

On both occasions, when I challenged these leaders on their approach, the suggestion that people management should be the number one priority was one that they found hard to accept given other pressures and priorities. This neglect leads to human potential going to waste every day.

You can't deny the link between job satisfaction and the way people feel about how their manager helps them get the job done.

In one of my favourite books, *Good Boss, Bad Boss* by Robert Sutton (author of *The No Asshole Rule*), Sutton refers to plenty of studies that show that poor bosses are a major cost to business and humanity. He quotes one study that found that '72% of workplace bullies were superiors who heaped abuse on subordinates.' What's more, 'a British study that tracked over 6000 civil servants for twenty years found that when their bosses criticised them unfairly, didn't listen to their problems and rarely offered praise, they suffered more angina, heart attacks and death from heart disease.'

Research aside, think about the good and bad managers you have worked for. Were you more productive when working for a good manager? Did you enjoy your job more and apply yourself with greater effort and commitment? So why is this compelling evidence and common sense often ignored in practice?

Our workplaces have evolved over more than a century of industrialisation to value managers more as 'doers of work' than 'enablers of others'. This reality is evidenced by the way we tend to:

- promote good technocrats or professionals into management roles because we want to give them headroom for pay increases and job-level advancement

- sacrifice several people who work for poor managers, in order to retain one person who is really good at what they do, rather than replace them with a manager who is good at leading others

- place inadequate attention on the development of people management skills and capability.

- lack feedback systems that project the voice of the employee to the manager and, even where they do exist, ignore employee feedback, so that great cynicism arises about such mechanisms and their value

- put limited or little focus on team performance in our organisations.

The lack of commitment to people management as a top priority is a huge contributor to the gap that organisations experience between their current performance and their potential.

I had the opportunity to share ideas with Sir Ralph Norris, former CEO of the Commonwealth Bank of Australia (and architect of the success the bank experienced well after his retirement), to discuss his thoughts on what makes a high-performing organisation.

Ralph was very clear on the importance of expecting excellence from managers of people and leveraging employee feedback as a core aspect of making the judgement. He said, 'Changing the culture in your business can be quick if you step up to, confront and if necessary change the management in areas of the business that are not performing or behaving to expectation.'

People managers are the critical nodes in the network that connect people with the purpose of an organisation and align what they do and how they do it with strategic priorities and ambitions. Your business is only ever as good as your management team.

When I became Managing Director at Microsoft Australia, I held people management meetings three or four times a year with our 100 people managers. This meeting was one of the most important in our business. As the management cohort got stronger, so did our business performance.

Early on I declared that being an effective people manager was to be added to every manager's job objectives (at that point it was not even on the list) and to become the number one priority and influence over their performance rating. In other words, the manager's performance rating would be tied to their feedback results in our annual employee opinion survey.

There was an outcry in the meeting: 'How can you do this to us when we have so many other things to do?'

I said, 'Your role as people managers is the most important function in the business, and if you don't think you have the time available to do it well, see your manager (or ultimately me) and we will help you reprioritise.'

Fortunately, I never needed to help in the prioritisation process.

At Xero, I continued the practice of holding people leader meetings three times a year. I'd conduct the meetings three times each time to make sure I was able to meet with all our people leaders (more than 700 of them) in their time zone. Each people leader meeting focused on business performance and on developing people leader skills in areas such as crucial conversations and career planning for their people.

Put the right people in the right roles

Continuous change results in the need to adjust organisation structure and move people into new roles and out of old roles. Also inevitably, some people who once suited the role they played in the organisation will no longer be a great fit.

> *I warn CEOs that at least one-third of their direct reports will become misfits if they are making a significant change to strategy. The next third will relish or be a better fit with the change, while the final third will stay or need to go, depending on the extent of the change in direction.*

Remember, organisations don't change unless people do!

In start-ups it is not unusual to cycle a number of people through various roles over time as the needs of the business change, and as the capabilities of the person needed to perform the role change. This often applies to company founders, who can become a 'misfit' in their own organisation if their management capabilities don't evolve to enable them to run a bigger and more established business.

At ninemsn, the head of technology and development role changed several times in the first five years, as did the person performing it, as we transitioned from start-up to emerging business to established business.

I worked closely with the CEO of a major entertainment company during their transition from their origins as a merger of three founder-led businesses into a subsidiary of a major international corporation. The journey required very different capabilities and culture as the changes in strategy and operations made misfits of once-effective executives. The willingness by the CEO to make the tough calls to ensure the right people filled the right role was key to the progress made on the change journey.

At Microsoft Australia, our growth agenda required our executive team to collaborate more closely than ever. This suited some members of my team, but not all. One very control-oriented executive found it hard to open up to challenge or inspection by others. The executive made frequent reference to 'my business' and 'my organisation', and 'me' rather than 'we'. Ultimately, we parted ways because that mindset did not suit the changes in strategy and cross-team collaboration we were keen to implement.

The constant evolution of organisation structure and people is a feature of leading and adapting to change that requires good hiring processes and decisions. When it comes to hiring people, the best advice I've been given includes:

- Don't ask hypothetical questions, such as 'How would you...?' Ask for responses that lean on real experience, such as 'Describe a situation when you...'

- If you aren't sure about the hiring decision, it's probably a no-hire, or the process demands further exploration of what is causing doubt.

Know who you would hate to lose

Leaders who care about people make a point of knowing the best talent in their organisation. If treated as a priority, there are simple ways to do this with support of HR. A process that works well to focus on the quality of talent in an organisation is the nine-box matrix of performance and potential. (The nine-box matrix 'how to' guide in the Must-Do Toolbox explains how this works.)

Creating the matrix requires the performance and potential of everyone to be assessed and documented annually. A six-monthly review is even better. This exercise turns quality of talent into data that can be analysed and given ongoing attention. The process, if coordinated, can provide management teams with an opportunity to collectively review the performance of people in their peers' departments. The exercise also helps draw issues to the surface and create accountability for each manager to address performance issues in their teams.

Knowing your high-performing people is an important aspect of developing and managing talent. This focus means being clear about the people you would hate to lose (HTL). These people should get priority access to training and development and have opportunities to meet and be mentored by more senior people in the organisation.

When considering your HTL people, it's important that their behaviour is consistent with the values and expectations you aspire to, so you promote role models rather than people who achieve objectives regardless of the impact on others around them.

Decide how often you want to have a conversation about top talent with members of your team and ask them to be ready to discuss it with you on those occasions. You can also peer review with your team members to make sure you get a third-party perspective of who the HTL people are and how satisfied they are to continue working in your organisation.

Final words on Being and Character

Character is deeply embedded in who you are as a human being. Being self-aware and conscious of your thinking and actions is key to authentically demonstrating the three Must-Dos we have touched on in Part II.

Truth is found in how others perceive you. Seeking feedback and being open to hearing things you might not want to hear is important for aligning the inner you with the one other people experience.

Understand that success comes through others around you, especially people who support you, and that helping others to be the best they can be is what leadership is all about, regardless of your role.

Developing character is a journey with no final destination. Learning how your character is perceived and influences others is an investment worth making. Doing the work to understand how your life and work experiences and influences have shaped your subconscious is another great investment to make, so you can be more conscious in applying the three Must-Dos.

Coaching can help a lot here. In my experience, a great way to assess someone's character is to consider how coachable they are.

Coachable people are open minded and:

- willing to accept the views of others as their reality, even if they disagree with them

- willing to change their opinion or course based on the suggestions of others

- proactively seek and accept feedback and ways to learn and improve

- listen actively without being defensive.

Being coachable is an attribute that accelerates character development and is worth understanding better. Useful resources available include the book *Coachability: The Leadership Superpower* by Kevin Wilde.

In Part III we move from Being to Doing and consider how character plays out day to day through our words and actions.

Chapter summary

If you want people to think you care, you need to show you care by being at their service and making it safe for them to speak their truth.

Questions to ask yourself (or to ask others about you):

- Am I willing to sacrifice what is good for me in the best interests of the organisation or team?

- Do I create a safe environment for people to challenge me and speak their truth, even if I won't like what they have to say?

- Do I demonstrate care for our people, customers and external stakeholders?

Recommended actions:

- Be clear about why you lead your organisation and team, and demonstrate that it is 'not just about you'.

- Go out of your way to make it safe and thank people who challenge you.

- Think like a head coach, investing time and energy to build a great team and talent around you.

- Don't allow persistently weak people leaders to stay in their role.

Refer to the Must-Do Toolbox:

- Nine-Box talent management process.

PART III

'DOING' THROUGH WORDS AND ACTIONS

In Part III we explore the 'Doing' domain, the words and actions we use to lead and respond to change.

	Must-Do actions
BEING *Character*	1. Apply the <u>right mindset</u>
	2. Be <u>self-aware</u>
	3. <u>Care about people</u>
DOING *Words and actions*	4. Seek <u>clarity</u>
	5. Drive <u>alignment</u>
	6. Focus on <u>performance</u>
	7. <u>Have difficult conversations</u>
	8. <u>Make hard choices</u>

Another way to think about Doing is that it contains the element of executing strategy or, as I like to think of it, *what we need to do today to create the future we desire*. Without 'what we need to do today', strategy is no more than aspiration. Without long-term aspiration or intent, actions today will most likely lack alignment with a clear future.

If you don't want to change something, you don't need a strategy. The following Must-Dos comprise the elements of executing strategy:

- **Must-Do #4: Seek clarity**. Things are never 100 per cent clear, but doing the best you can to provide clarity of purpose, ambition, priorities and behaviours is a foundation of success.

- **Must-Do #5: Drive alignment.** Alignment of resources (people, money, technology) with priorities, which is often the missing link and where execution commonly falls down.

- **Must-Do #6. Focus on performance**. Commit to continuously review progress, and to decide whether choices made and actions taken require adjustment. Review organisational, team and individual performance.

Must-Do #s 4, 5 and 6 shape and inform each other in a continuous cycle of learning and change over time. The final two, Must-Do #s 7 and 8, sit at the heart of execution and change (see figure III.1).

- **Must-Do #7: Have difficult conversations**. Words spoken and written are all we have to express our intentions and actions. The pace of change is defined by the frequency, speed and quality of the conversations we have. The drive for clarity, alignment and focus on performance requires that difficult conversations are initiated and concluded in a productive way.

- **Must-Do #8: Make hard choices**. You are your decisions, and making hard choices lies at the heart of the Must-Do actions to seek clarity, drive alignment and focus on performance.

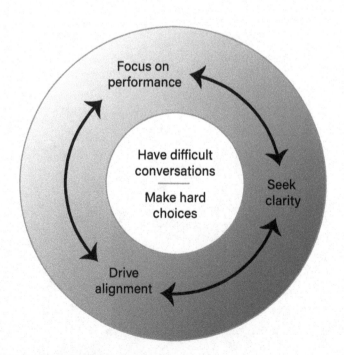

Figure III.1: interplay of Must-Do actions

CHAPTER 8

MUST-DO #4: SEEK CLARITY

There's a lot we don't know about what lies ahead. Uncertainty surrounds changes we initiate, such as a new purpose or vision for the future, or external impacts of an economic downturn or global pandemic. In the face of uncertainty, we need to do the best we can to create clarity that helps anchor the actions we take.

Clarity is most needed in purpose, ambition, priorities and behaviour. Seeking clarity means being conscious about what is uncertain and unclear and keeping an eye out for any signals that can help give you confidence that you are on the right track or need to adjust course.

Clarity of purpose

When Apple Computer removed 'Computer' from its name, it signalled a big change in the company's purpose, from making personal computers to a much broader domain that included phones and other internet-based devices and services.

As Xero grew from a start-up to a global small business platform, our vision evolved from 'delivering beautiful cloud accounting software' to 'being the most trusted and insightful small business platform'.

While vision statements can sound like simple statements of intent, in times of change they are an important guide to prioritisation and making the right investment choices. They also provide people with the big-picture purpose or meaning of their work. Reflecting on why you do what you do is a critical protection against irrelevance in the future.

In the past, vision and mission statements that defined an organisation's purpose weren't reviewed often and didn't change significantly over the course of a few years. Sticking with the status quo also meant avoiding the frustrating wordsmithing sessions this process can demand.

> **In changing times, a purpose with diminishing relevance is a major alarm bell.**

The importance of being clear about purpose became intensely obvious to me in my role as CEO of ninemsn. About nine months into the journey, ninemsn was not a happy place. We were burning a lot of cash, and there was a lot of infighting going on. Our website and its performance were ordinary at best, and the Board of Directors were not impressed.

To get to the bottom of our dysfunction, I held a company meeting to better understand how people were feeling about the business and where we were heading. I asked people to rate their overall satisfaction with working at ninemsn as a score out of 10. When we collected and counted the individual votes on Post-it notes, the average score was 4 out of 10. Not good.

Despite the enviable work environment with funky offices in Paddington, open air workspaces, a courtyard that featured a beautiful old oak tree, and an open invitation to innovate and create new media experiences pretty much at will, people were not satisfied working at ninemsn.

Initially on receiving this feedback I had to compose myself. My first reaction was to think that I was surrounded by a bunch of spoilt young people who had no idea how good they had it. With an average age of 28, most people had never experienced a market crash or downturn, and just didn't know how lucky they were. After permitting myself a private, internal vent, I began the journey of listening to what had caused the negative sentiment.

After much deliberation, which included discussion of highly strategic issues like the lack of a shower on site for those wanting to exercise during the day, we landed on a very clear and consistent message.

> **People were not clear about our purpose or where ninemsn was heading, and as a result were not sure they were contributing or working on things that really mattered.**

This feedback from our people had a big impact on me, because it highlighted the importance of aligning people with a clear purpose or the 'big picture'. This was something I knew but had not adequately appreciated. It led to a concerted effort by my executive team to define what ninemsn should be, could be and, even more important, what we were *not* going to be.

Up to that point ninemsn was trying to do too much. We were 'too rich' in resources, which meant that at Board and executive level we had the luxury of kidding ourselves that we could do more than we really could. People inside the business at all levels were concerned we were doing too much and doing nothing well.

It fell to me as CEO and the management team to have the difficult conversations and make the hard choices that brought greater clarity of purpose and better allocation of resources towards what ninemsn could do well.

We decided to exit several categories of business including travel (a local version of Expedia that we had in development) and news origination (we had journalists located around the country thinking we could compete with the likes of Fairfax and News Corp). We also gradually shut down Sidewalk (our first and probably best-designed website), a local directory that was years ahead of its time and had a vision that many local search and review sites fulfil today. We moved more of our focus to building the ninemsn network and aggregating content provided by partners.

Ultimately, the stack of 10 business plans ninemsn started out with was narrowed down to the three or four things we could execute well.

The search for clarity of purpose characterised a series of very difficult conversations and hard choices to stop doing things and reassign resources to focus on the few things we could do well.

Over the next 12 months ninemsn evolved into an online network of content and services aggregated from a wide range of partners. We limited origination of content to a few areas where we had the skills and resources to do things well. The positive outcomes from the pain we went through to gain focus and clarity of purpose made it well worth the effort.

One year later I reran the employee satisfaction survey that previously resulted in the 4 out of 10 score. The new survey scored 8 out of 10, a significant increase resulting from driving clarity of purpose.

During that 12-month period, as we drove alignment with purpose across the business, we turned over about 35 per cent of our staff. As we became clearer about our purpose, people who were not committed or excited about the direction we were taking decided to move on to other things.

Another significant benefit of clarity of purpose was the opportunity to replace those who left the business with people who really wanted to be on the journey.

In his book *Start with Why*, Simon Sinek addresses the importance of clarity of purpose that inspires people to do the work they do.

Too often we jump into action before we have adequately considered why we are doing what we do, and deeper definition of the problem we're trying to solve. Unless we start with why in design or in response to change, we cannot expect the right outcome, as we have not adequately defined the problem we're trying to solve.

Spending time pursuing clarity of purpose reduces the risk that what you do becomes less meaningful over time to those you serve, helping to avoid eventual irrelevance and death.

Checking in on the question of why we do what we do as part of the strategy and annual planning process is important, as is refining and being clear about your value proposition or unique sales proposition (USP). I recommend asking the following questions as part of this process:

- What business are we in?

- What is our value proposition?

- How do we know that customers care?

- Are we growing revenue? (If your revenue growth is slowing, you are or may be in decline.)

- How might new entrants disrupt us?

- How would we disrupt ourselves?

- Could we add more value by changing our vision or mission to go upstream, downstream or into new business/areas?

- What outside opinions have been sought about these questions?

It is important to have this conversation unrestricted by the views and biases of senior people, or by the thinking or attitudes that are hostage to past success. For example, if there's a founder or previous leader in the room who might be confronted by the discussion, how can that be managed?

> *It is crucial to ask if there is anything impeding a full and open conversation about purpose, or the need to change or stop doing things that enabled success in the past.*

Burning ambition

One of the best bosses I had during my career at IBM was Ravi Marwaha, a smart and energetic executive who left an indelible mark on me. Aside from Ravi's great capacity and energy, he took me under his wing and helped me on many occasions when I was confronted with difficult issues and challenges; in fact, some of those difficult challenges came to me thanks to Ravi.

In one of our first meetings, I was talking Ravi through a particular marketing program I was developing that fell way short of his expectations of what was possible. I became defensive, explaining why his aspiration and expectations were impossible and unreasonable.

Ravi was getting fed up with me. He allowed a bit of a pause in the conversation and then looked me straight in the eyes, raised his voice and emphatically said: 'Steve!...Stop!...Don't tell me it can't be done! Come back and tell me what we need to do to make it happen.'

I went back to my desk convinced Ravi was being unreasonable. Nevertheless, he was the boss so I thought I'd better listen to him and respond accordingly. As I started to think about a more ambitious objective, his words, 'tell me what we need to do to make it happen', kept ringing in my head. As I reflected, I realised that many of the constraints I saw could be overcome if I got support from Ravi and the organisation to change aspects of the way we did things.

I went back to see Ravi a few days later with a more ambitious goal and a list of things IBM would need to do to achieve these greater aspirations. Ravi reviewed the list with me and made decisions on which ones we, or others, could or couldn't do for organisational or financial reasons. As we concluded the meeting, we ended up with a much more ambitious goal than my original proposal, and a set of actions to enable us to achieve it.

This interaction changed me. It made me more ambitious and it made me think bigger. I appreciated Ravi for showing me that often what seems impossible is indeed possible, and I think of him every time I ask someone I work with to think about what is possible.

Gary Hamel, the author of *What Matters Now*, refers to organisations having 'ambition deficit disorder (ADD)'. Ambition is so important because it represents a determination for things to be different and better. It is a foundation for innovation.

There's little chance of changing things for the better without real ambition and asking what is possible.

Entrepreneur Peter Diamandis refers to the ambition of disrupters in his blogs as having a 'Massively Transformative Purpose' (MTP). 'Can you appreciate that we're alive during an age when individuals are pulling off what was once only possible by the greatest nations? We're living during a time when astonishing surprises are materializing at an ever-increasing rate. When seemingly insane or science fiction ideas are routinely becoming real and commonplace...'

The power of purpose and ambition go together to motivate people to pursue and create a new future. Change without clear purpose and ambition is hard to realise. Too often a business planning process starts with preconceived or limiting consideration of what is possible. Parameters are set (usually top down) based on past performance and market and competitor growth (what others did in the past), rather than on curiosity of what might be possible.

A planning and budgeting process should always start with the very powerful question, *What is possible?*

Clearly the caveat here is that you do smart and sustainable things to achieve those ambitious goals.

At Xero, we had a big appetite for growth given the opportunity presented by further driving adoption of cloud accounting. To that end we executed a range of meaningful strategic actions with that long-term ambition in mind.

> **Clear ambition is a driver of growth, efficiency and extraordinary performance.**

Priorities and focus

Prioritising is one of the toughest functions leaders and their teams confront. Today the pressure to prioritise is greater than ever, because every day there are more and more opportunities to do new things and at the same time increasing demands to improve efficiency. Doing too much is an impediment to good execution. The saying 'Ideas are a commodity; good execution is not' sums it up!

Lack of prioritisation causes serious problems:

- People constantly complain they are trying to do too much.

- Things go wrong or fall through the cracks when they shouldn't.

- The quality of products and services declines or is not good enough.

Prioritisation is hard because it means making hard choices, such as:

- exiting businesses that made you successful in the past

- not pursuing good ideas because of a lack of resources

- ceasing services to customers because they are no longer commercially viable.

Steve Jobs was a 'savant' when it came to prioritising. He exemplified leading with purpose, ambition and obsessive focus, and he demanded that those around him align with that purpose and that it transcends individual ambition or self-interest. He very clearly signalled to all in Apple about what was important and expected.

Jobs set a great example by having the courage to say no to good ideas in the pursuit of focus and good execution. Asked about this by Bloomberg, he said, 'It comes from saying no to 1000 things to make sure we don't get on the wrong track or try to do too much. We're always thinking about new markets we could enter, but it's only by saying no that you can concentrate on the things that are really important.'

The decision to kill the Apple Newton handheld device was one such courageous decision about which I questioned Steve directly. We had thousands of developers around the world building applications for the device who would be impacted by the decision to terminate it. Steve's one-line email response to me was: 'We must focus on saving the Mac.'

This focus (and courage) saved Apple and built the platform for the success that followed.

Most of us don't like saying no to good people who do good work and have good ideas. It's far easier to say 'a bit of yes' to many things than it is to say no and only pursue a few things that you commit to do well. Prioritisation means making hard choices and having the difficult conversations that we often avoid or delay having. If you don't prioritise, you end up doing too much, and lose clarity.

The downstream effect of asking people to do too much is lack of accountability. It becomes okay for people to do less than expected, as it was never realistic they could do what was expected in the first place. Rather than a 'culture of commitment', a 'culture of best endeavours' becomes the norm, and with that comes a significant impact on quality of execution and business performance.

A great way to drive clarity is to have a well-structured one- or two-day team meeting that focuses on the pressing issues and priorities for action. It's a good way to fast-track 80 per cent of the most important things you derive from a more complete strategy process that considers the wide range of influences and change that can impact an organisation in the future.

> *Good strategy is defining 'what we need to do today to create the future we desire'.*

In this process, the right people come together to answer the question, What are the top five things we need to be doing now to achieve our aspirations?

Note that this process assumes there is reasonable clarity of purpose and ambition, which is not always the case. Make sure to check this before people answer the question. If not, go back a step to get clear about the team's purpose and ambition.

After each person has discussed their top five things, these are ordered into similar groups and prioritised by the group. What results is a top five for the group. Invariably the top five emerge very clearly and from there an action plan can be defined to address them.

On one occasion at a meeting I was facilitating, while we reviewed the output from the top 25 or so people of a technology business I was advising, the CEO paused and said, 'This is bullshit!'

I asked him why.

'Because the emergent themes of concern could have related to any company.'

I replied, 'First, yes they could, because in my experience 80 per cent of the issues that get in the way of executing strategy are not specific to the industry you operate in. In other words, what you do might make you different from others; however, the things that get in the way are common to most organisations. They are about execution (the how) rather than intent (the what). Second, it's your people raising these as the things you need to action to achieve your goals, not me.'

> For a sample agenda and notes on how to run this style of meeting, refer to the 'Fast-track clarity of priorities' guide in the Must-Do Toolbox.

Expectations of behaviour

In the early days of building ninemsn, dysfunctional behaviours were common because we were a new business without clear standards. A meeting of our people was like a scene from the cantina in the first *Star Wars* movie that brought people together from across the galaxy.

The new and convergent nature of the online media industry meant that most start-ups blended people with diverse backgrounds in information technology, media and communications, and consulting. The resulting cultural diversity was a necessary and appreciated part of the company's culture; however, the business at that time suffered because there was no common understanding or consistent commitment to how we worked and treated each other.

In a memorable meeting, the ninemsn executive team was reviewing a significant project failure. The project team members were speaking from the front of the boardroom, and my executive team was seated around the boardroom table. As the team began their presentation, one of the executives on my team slammed his fist on the table and shouted, 'I knew that wouldn't work!'

I was shocked by his outburst, and asked, 'Did you tell them that you thought they would fail?'

'No I did not!' he replied.

'Why didn't you tell them?' I asked.

'I didn't tell them because the last time I tried to tell them that something they were doing wouldn't work, they told me to piss off and mind my own business!'

This behaviour was a huge impediment to our development. Highly skilled and creative people in the business were not sharing their opinions and knowledge, except when it was too late. I described the behaviour like this: 'Our culture reflects someone sitting on a riverbank, happily waving to people rowing a canoe down a fast-flowing river towards a dangerous waterfall they know is around the bend.' Nasty emails, with a 'shoot first, ask questions later' tone, were regularly sent from one person to another when things went wrong.

The culture we inherited from people joining ninemsn from traditional media companies was technically skilled and creative, but extremely defensive and focused on their own function or content area of the network. The inherent culture was territorial and had little tolerance for being questioned by anyone outside their direct line of reporting regarding the way they were going about doing their jobs.

If one content category outperformed another, they would proudly announce that 'we generated more traffic than they did last month'. A real competitor of our business was seldom mentioned. It seemed that the real competitor was another publishing team in the ninemsn organisation, rather than a rival publisher.

Given our strategy to be a network with each content area referring traffic to others of the network, ninemsn needed consistency in branding and navigation and strong linkages across all our websites. We needed to provide a seamless and consistent experience to our customers.

The travel category needed to establish linkages to finance ('get a personal loan') and sport ('travel to New Zealand to watch the Bledisloe Cup') in order to enhance the customer relationship and broaden usage of the network. This required much greater collaboration and cooperation among our people, and a common approach to developing websites.

The behavioural issues in the early days were huge obstacles to the development of a strong, well-functioning online business. We needed a different culture to survive and thrive, as do many organisations now that are still too functionally oriented in silos, and not collaborating or connecting enough to best serve their customers.

With the business deep in the process of finding a winning and profitable formula, establishing clear behavioural standards was a huge priority. We decided to involve our people in the process of defining the values and behavioural standards of the organisation. We ran workshops to identify the positive and negative aspects of existing behaviour and to lay down a framework for the desired behaviours of the organisation. We engaged people we saw as 'role models' in the process.

The workshops led to the development of corporate values that identified the positive behavioural attributes necessary for success long term, and the values necessary to counter the dysfunctional behaviours we were seeing.

An important value that emerged from the outburst in the meeting described earlier was 'We share knowledge', with associated behaviours:

- We are committed to teamwork and shared knowledge.

- We demonstrate open and frank communication.

- We speak directly to each other when we have issues.

- We are upfront and willing to address issues directly.

This was the first time I was involved in a 'bottom-up' definition of company values, with people in the business identifying the dysfunction we needed to stop. This approach was more effective than having people at the top come up with the values and mandate them.

A business needs to live by values and behaviours that resonate with day-to-day work life, and address the dysfunction that gets in the way of people doing their best work.

The following are the ninemsn values and behaviours as they evolved from the initial process.

- *We value and care for our customers, clients, partners and shareholders*

- *We are passionate about our media and strive to lead the industry*

- *We think network first*

- *We are open, honest and respectful of others*

- *We are self critical and committed to improvement*

Once values and behaviours are clearly established, it is important to reinforce them when hiring, promoting and exiting people from the business.

Values can, and often need to, evolve over time as an organisation changes. It's worth reviewing the values every couple of years and considering whether any changes are required. Giving and receiving regular feedback on how we live the values is fundamental to making them real. The feedback should be integrated into the performance review process to make it effective.

Another practice I encourage is the development of a team code, which is a behavioural code specific to a team that defines how they work together. This is helpful because individuals and teams across an organisation differ in the kind of work they do, and in the way they work.

The Must-Do Toolbox contains a guide on the steps required to develop a team code and live by it.

Final words on clarity

A commitment to achieving clarity of purpose, ambition, priorities and behaviours is critical to a great change program and teamwork. It's okay to call out what is not clear and continue to subject that area of concern to further testing, consideration and change. Clarity is rarely static; it evolves and emerges from the interaction with Must-Do #5 of the 'Doing' domain, *Drive Alignment*, which we explore next.

Chapter summary

Despite many things being unknown or changing, it is important to seek clarity as best you can from what you learn and experience.

Questions to ask yourself (or to ask others about you):

- Does our team have clarity of purpose?
- Is our team ambitious?
- Does our team have clear priorities and focus?
- Does our team have clear expectations of how team members should behave?

Recommended actions:

- Check in and review the purpose of your organisation/ team every year; is it still relevant or does it need to evolve?
- Ask yourself and others on your team 'what is possible?' in setting your plans, rather than using last year's performance as a base.
- Don't accept lack of clarity of priorities. Invest the time to get as clear as possible.
- Identify the values and behaviours you aspire to and make sure to provide feedback to each other regarding how they are collectively and individually lived.

Refer to the Must-Do Toolbox:

- Fast-track clarity of priorities.
- Develop a team code and live it.

CHAPTER 9

MUST-DO #5: DRIVE ALIGNMENT

I was taught how to develop a strategic plan as a first-time manager at IBM. My boss, Brian Scott, made clear, in his strong Scottish accent, 'Steve, yuu must have a plun!'

I was also taught how to set objectives for people and how to run performance reviews. What I did not learn until many years later was how to drive real alignment between strategic plans and the work individuals do. I believe most leaders do an inadequate job on alignment because they don't appreciate the importance of it or lack the capability to do it.

As individuals, alignment of our day-to-day actions with our intentions is also where lack of process or discipline means we fall short of the expectations we set for ourselves.

The missing link

The Board and management of David Jones were committed to great customer service as a strategic priority. That commitment didn't translate to the experience a friend of mine had when shopping at the department store. About to purchase $10 000 worth of clothes, he was asked to pay $100 for alterations to a pair of trousers he wanted to buy. My friend was annoyed and told the shop assistant that he'd be going elsewhere.

The shop assistant asked him to wait a moment and returned after some time with his supervisor's approval to waive the alteration charge.

An otherwise positive shopping experience was soured by this interaction and prompted me to share this customer's experience with a senior executive of the company. The executive slapped his forehead with exasperation and said the shop assistant was 'silly' for not waiving the charge in the first place.

But whose fault was this?

Fault lay with senior management. The shop assistant fell victim to misalignment between the company's big-picture intentions to deliver great customer service and the day-to-day expectations of their people at the storefront.

Too often misalignment exists between the world a CEO and Board think they are creating, and the reality of people at the front line of the organisation. This lack of alignment stops the execution of strategy dead.

The work on strategy often ends at defining purpose, goals and priorities (the relatively easy part, about 20 per cent of the task) and doesn't drive hard enough to ensure the real alignment of resources and actions required to execute the strategy.

The hardest 80 per cent of executing strategy is driving the alignment of people, technology and resources with *how* it is intended to achieve goals and aspirations.

In the past, alignment was not the challenge it is today, because the pace of change was not as fast.

Leaders must obsessively drive alignment between their strategic intentions and the day-to-day experience of people at every level of the organisation. This obsession includes removing barriers that exist or arise for people doing the work.

While many people have basic skills in strategy setting, there is a significant capability gap in the skills and discipline needed to align execution with strategy.

The CEO of an organisation in the consulting industry proudly told me that driving alignment across his 5000-people organisation was going to be his number two priority.

'What's your number one priority?' I asked.

'Spending time with my clients,' he replied.

'Don't you have people working for you that can handle that?' I asked.

'Yes,' he said. 'But I want to send a clear signal to the organisation that clients come first.'

I replied, 'Every minute you spend driving stronger alignment means 5000 people are likely to be more effective in your organisation serving clients. Your time meeting with one client has less impact and leverage than you have as CEO driving alignment of 5000 people. I think you have two important priorities the wrong way around.'

Leaders and their teams must grind through the alignment challenges and issues with conviction to make strategy execution real. Alignment is the capability that extends strategy to *what we need to do today to create the future we desire*. Strategy without alignment is hit and miss or simply hopes and dreams.

Alignment is a process that defines who needs to do what, who needs to help, what resources are allocated and what choices are made in the face of resource constraints.

I was introduced to the process of alignment called level order planning when I was Managing Director of Microsoft Australia. It significantly changed my approach to strategy and planning.

Drive alignment with level order planning

Level order planning (LOP) is a process by which strategy is translated into priorities, objectives and actions that are:

- clearly worded

- clear in the accountability of identified leaders and supporters

- measurable

- cascaded level by level through the organisation as the top-level strategies and objectives are translated into specific lower-level actions

- synchronised across the organisation to ensure that actions that rely on cross-functional cooperation and collaboration produce the desired outcome.

I spoke with a group of CEOs in a roundtable session, sharing my experiences and views on leadership in changing times. Tom Daunt, the CEO of ALDI Australia, the fast-growing and successful supermarket business, attended that meeting.

Since opening its first store in 2001 in Sydney, ALDI Australia's performance has been phenomenal. By 2023 it operated 570 stores across the country and directly employed more than 13 500 people. ALDI's revenue had grown to over $10 billion in 2022.

Tom got in touch with me a few days after our session and asked to have a coffee and talk further about the one thing I spoke about that struck his interest: driving alignment and level order planning.

While Tom was confident ALDI Australia had a clear strategy, he was very concerned that the execution of the strategy was not as effective as it could be. Top down, Tom and his team had developed and agreed on seven key strategies and 11 objectives. These were tested and aligned with the four quadrants of the Balanced scorecard.

The strategy was clear and sound. The issue confronting Tom was that, bottom up, each of his team members and their functions was pursuing a total of an additional 120 objectives and 120 projects for their parts of the business.

Tom's initiative to do this stocktake was impressive and demonstrated his personal drive for alignment. The additional objectives and projects implied support for executing the strategy, but were not explicitly aligned, prioritised and connected across the business. Put simply, a lot of activity (in fact too much) was going on, without clear alignment with executing the strategy.

Figure 9.1 shows the high-level top-down strategies and objectives agreed by Tom's direct reports, along with the additional 120 functional objectives and 120 projects. The reality was that the two did not explicitly align, and too many things were being pursued.

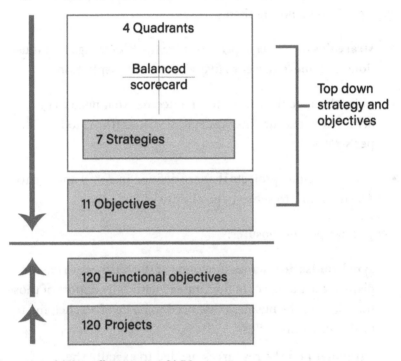

Figure 9.1: driving alignment at ALDI

The line across the middle of the chart represents potential misalignment in converting strategy to execution. I helped Tom confirm his concern that a vital step in the strategy process was missing, and that level order planning would help address the problem.

The next step was for Tom to bring together the top team and next layer of management to explicitly define the cross-business actions needed to execute the most important (top-down) seven strategies and

11 objectives. These cross-business actions would become functional objectives and priority projects executed in a synchronised way. The resources required to execute would be prioritised over the bottom-up objectives and projects or lead to a healthy debate about the relative importance of the bottom-up projects.

Figure 9.2 shows how level order planning requires top teams and the business to explicitly define the *strategies – objectives – actions* required to execute the strategy, and that these inform what happens at each level of the organisation, noting that:

- **strategies** or strategic priorities are the BIG things that must get done to achieve three- to five-year goals or aspirations

- **objectives** are the nearer-term outcomes that need to be achieved to execute the strategic priorities (three to five per strategy)

- **actions** include projects that are defined in detail and are to be executed now to achieve the objectives.

This top-down process ensures:

1. **synchronisation** across functions of the business to ensure plans are set to execute the strategy with full support of those functions of the business that need to be involved, helping to bridge functional silos

2. **agreement** on the resources needed to execute the strategy and commitment of all parties to contribute the resources needed

3. **clarity** for middle management of where they should focus, rather than a raft of high-level expectations from senior management without qualifying the resources and alignment needed to make the strategy real

4. **prioritisation** of the important actions required to execute the strategy.

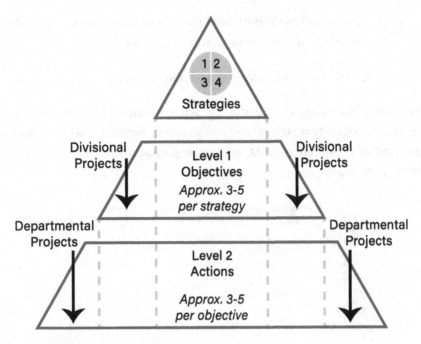

Figure 9.2: level order planning

In Tom's memo to his team, he outlined the following objectives of the level order planning process:

- Review our current business goals, strategies and priorities to reconfirm them or amend them as necessary.

- Strengthen alignment between the actions we are taking throughout the business and the strategic priorities we select to pursue in each of our balanced scorecard quadrants.

- Ensure that we have the right focus on (and that we prioritise) the important actions needed to support our strategic priorities.

- Better design actions to address strategies requiring cross-departmental solutions.

- If possible, reduce the number of projects we pursue across the business with the aim of doing fewer things better, and allowing our teams to focus more on business performance within their existing responsibilities.

• Ensure our direct reports and their teams are fully engaged in our strategy and business planning process.

• Improve clarity of strategies and objectives.

Tom and his team also came up with a one-page summary and scorecard, an early sketch of which is shown in figure 9.3, which became the unifying reference point for the organisation on what was most important to all.

ALDI AUSTRALIA – LEVEL 1 STRATEGY & OBJECTIVES

	STRATEGIES	OBJECTIVES	KPI	
FINANCIAL (f)	Optimise profitability for long term sustainability and market success	F1a) Achieve our Financial Forecasts across the business	Sales, Growth, Planning, RoB, Capital, etc	
CUSTOMER (c)	1. Offer market leading value – price, quality, range	C1a) Deliver an improved 'fresh' offer	Fresh Sales, Fresh %...	
	2. Deliver a customer experience they recommend to others	C2a) Consistently adhere to our chosen benchmarks for store environment, store standards and service	Mystery Shop, Net Promoter	
		C2b) Improve availability	Fresh Avail, NPS	
INTERNAL PROCESS (i)	1. Run the leanest, simplest, lowest cost structure feasible in our market	I1a) Improve standardisation of process and consistent application across Co.	{	{
	2. Optimise our store network – density, location, standard and size	I2a) Extend our global chophouse stores	{	{
		I2b) Optimise our network and plan for optimisation	{	{
PEOPLE (e)	1. Build a high performance culture, disciplined, results focused, supportive	P1a) Improve accountability and recognition	?	?
		P1b) Foster a 'Can do / Help' attitude	{	{
	2. Maintain high employee engagement and improve retention	P2a) Focus on recruitment and development	{	{
		P2b) Develop comprehensive HR strategy with key priorities	{	{

Figure 9.3: ALDI level one strategies and objectives

In 2023 Tom was promoted to a global leadership role as co-CEO of Aldi Sud, reflecting his success at ALDI Australia.

Level order planning is not easy and requires top-level focus and commitment to the process. The process gets more challenging as an organisation grows and becomes more complex. With that growth, alignment becomes an even more significant need.

There isn't one fixed way to do alignment. The process can be different and adapted to the nature of an organisation and its people. Whatever you do, make sure you find the right process to ensure that strategy in your organisation reflects *what needs to be done by your people today to create the future you desire.*

> **Make sure you have someone on the team with a strong business operations background or skill who is accountable to drive level order planning and the review process to ensure all team members are held accountable to deliver on their commitments.**

Working across functional silos

Functional silos have defined the shape of organisations for well over a century. These functions provide necessary focus on business processes with specific discipline and specialisation — for example, Finance and Sales. Unfortunately, silos are also major obstacles to change and transformation, particularly when their functional leaders operate with their own priorities rather than according to the needs of the organisation as a whole.

Functional silos must be overcome to achieve great customer service and meet their expectations to be known and treated as the centre of every interaction with the organisations they do business with.

> **Understanding and improving the customer experience and putting the customer 'at the centre' is fundamental to most change and transformation agendas. This outcome is hard to achieve because it demands overcoming the fragmentation caused by functional silos and partly explains why so few organisations have truly great customer service.**

How many interactions with a company or organisation do you recall that you'd rate highly?

Overcoming the functional silo challenge is why organisations initiate programs to 'unite as one', such as those I've experienced at many companies including Microsoft and Telstra.

Functional silos have also been at the source of fragmentation in business processes and IT systems, which make organisations vulnerable to disruption by smaller, more agile challengers.

Microsoft is one of the greatest software companies the world will see. However, for quite some time Microsoft underperformed as an internet company because the functional silos of product, marketing and field operations were inadequately connected.

I would often say to senior executives, that if a website was updated once every three years like a software package, Microsoft would be the best internet company in the world. I wanted to make the point that alignment between sales (revenue sources), marketing (audience and competitive analysis) and product (content and technology), was inadequate for the Microsoft internet business, and that we operated at cycles that were too slow to keep up with internet industry competitors. Microsoft's strong performance suggests this problem has been addressed in recent years.

Level order planning (cascading and calibrating strategic priorities and actions) helps connect functional silos to align with bigger-picture transformational goals, while continuing to bring their specialised functional skills to the table.

The product management process

Continuously delivering and refining products and services with changes in market opportunity and customer expectations is a big challenge. The evolution of software development to new, more agile methods supports a continuous loop of design, build, test for user feedback and refinement. The discipline to do this well is at the heart of the product management and development process.

Good product management involves strong collaboration across several functional areas such as marketing, sales, technology and development or manufacturing. That collaboration doesn't happen easily without clear alignment of these functions and their management with the big-picture purpose and priorities of the organisation.

As product management guru and author of *Inspired: How to create tech products customers love*, Marty Cagan, says, 'Product management is about insights and judgement, both of which require a sharp mind.' And on strong product culture, Cagan says, 'They know great products are the result of true collaboration'.

Different product management processes can exist in one organisation for different needs; for example, the process for a start-up or new product business can be different from one for an established or mature product business.

The need for a great Product Manager became clear to me in the early days of digital media when we were struggling to build an effective ninemsn home page. Our lead designer had produced a nice-looking home page, however it was lacking on most other important dimensions. The Sales function was not happy with the advertising opportunities on the page. The Marketing function was not happy with the branding and network navigation on the page. The Technology function didn't like the page because it was hard to build and maintain. Finance was not happy because we were failing to generate revenue as a network and we were burning a lot of cash.

I had a long chat with our design lead about the home page and the need for it to better reflect the overall purpose and needs of the business and each function of it. This required trade-offs in design. The process of getting alignment to optimise our home page for ninemsn's overall needs was going to take a lot of hard work, difficult conversations and hard choices.

Our designer opted out, saying that their interests were to do 'cool stuff', not 'corporate stuff', and that they didn't relish the task of negotiating with each function of ninemsn to achieve consensus on what the home page should look like. They weren't the right person to be the product manager so he and I agreed to part ways and did so amicably.

This experience helped me realise that ninemsn's business functions were so unclear and misaligned that I really couldn't delegate the task of building the new home page specifications to anyone. I had to personally product manage the task in partnership with Kim Anderson, who headed up ninemsn's marketing and content functions at the time.

> *The fascinating realisation about optimising the ninemsn home page was that every function had to sub-optimise or make sacrifices for what was right for the network or business as a whole.*

This notion of sub-optimising each function for the good of the whole was something we had to work through. The only way to do this was to make sure everyone saw the same big-picture purpose, priorities and ambition of the business. Each function needed to see the rewards in getting the home page right for the network holistically rather than in their functional silos.

Once Kim and I created the first aligned ninemsn home page specification, we were able to evolve a process over time, led by our next design lead, Megan Townley, which consistently produced home page changes and innovations that reflected the overall ninemsn network purpose and needs.

As we developed much clearer alignment with our purpose and priorities, the new home page and network innovations presented to the executive team were surprising, encouraging and exciting.

I learned that an effective product management function is best enabled when everyone involved sees the same purpose, priorities and ambition for the product or service being developed. The process needs someone with the skills to coordinate across the differing interests and conflicts that arise in the process.

See the Must-Do Toolbox for a process to assess the strength of your product management capability.

Multi-product and multi-geo organisations

Maintaining alignment within an organisation as it grows is a big challenge. The capability of organisation development is important to addressing this challenge, with a strong HR lead partnering with the CEO to evolve the organisation structure to meet emerging needs.

A start-up with one customer set and one product line can be straightforward to organise functionally by having in place the right leaders for sales, marketing, product, technology and other support functions.

As the business grows to one that serves multiple customer segments with multiple products, organisation development becomes much more challenging due to the need to operate some form of matrix organisation structure.

At Xero introducing the matrix was challenging, especially in the domain of sales and marketing. Chief Customer Officer Rachael Powell had the big job of leading the program we called 'One Xero', which brought our four regional sales and marketing organisations under one global umbrella. Up to that point, each region had their own way of working, and as a result we had four voices lobbying the product groups regarding their customer needs. This situation made it very tough for the product teams to align around the company's highest priorities.

We also had four ways of interacting with and managing existing and new customers and subscale information technology systems to support sales operations.

Rachael did a great job establishing the global sales and marketing functions that would oversee the systems, tools and processes of those functions, so we would have the consistency and efficiency of approach that was required as we continued to scale.

The sales and marketing leaders of each region still reported to their Region executive, and also reported dotted line to their Global sales or marketing functional lead. The Global sales and marketing functions became the primary interface to our Product organisation.

The truth about the matrix

I've often heard negative comments about matrix organisation structures: they don't work, are too complex and/or confuse accountability. Some of the negative comments suggest that the matrix takes away control from key customer-facing business units or product divisions. That said, I don't know of a better way to organise a multi-customer and multi-product company, which is probably why the matrix is used by most successful global technology companies. If there is a better, easier way, I'm keen to hear about it!

The matrix organisation model is designed to:

- ensure consistency and efficiency of common cross-business functions and processes

- ensure that *two functional lines of thought and discipline* are applied when operating a business with multiple products and services provided to multiple customer segments. For these organisations it is vital that both a customer and a product business view is reflected in strategy, planning and execution.

In figure 9.4, the Education Product Manager is a key person in both the Education Customer-Facing Business Unit and the Product Business Unit. The Education Product Manager relies on plans and budgets being aligned for both sides of the matrix.

The discussion in matrix organisations is often, 'Who is the hard-line boss vs dotted line boss?' of the person in the middle of the matrix; in other words, which side of the matrix takes priority?

If misalignment in expectations exists between the customer-facing unit and the product unit, the matrix model won't work well (neither will the business under any model). It can leave the Education Product Manager feeling like 'the meat in the sandwich', and deferring to the person who is their 'hard' reporting line manager.

If product and customer expectations are aligned through a solid planning process, the matrix works well and the question as to who is the 'hard' vs 'dotted' line boss of the Education Product Manager is of less concern and frequency.

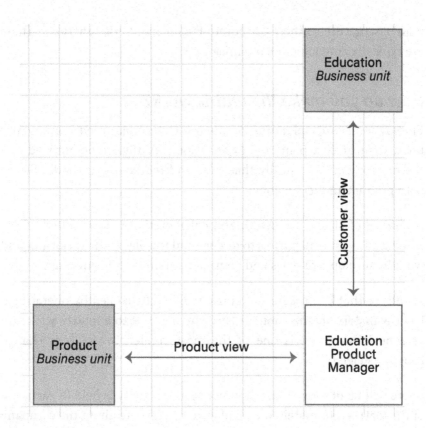

Figure 9.4: a typical matrix structure

Both sides of the matrix are involved in reviewing the performance of the person that connects them in the matrix. Hard line reporting is best assigned to the side of the matrix that has most day-to-day contact with the person in the middle. That's not a strict rule.

Where are matrix organisations a good fit?

The matrix organisation works best in larger or growing organisations that have multiple product lines of business and several customer types or segments.

Where would you avoid a matrix?

Organisations with a range of businesses that have little or no interdependency in customer or product set should limit the use of a matrix structure to their Corporate Finance and HR functions. These are typically conglomerate organisations.

How do you make the matrix work?

Employ level order planning or whatever good planning method you know to make sure plans and expectations are aligned on both sides of the matrix, and specifically that sales and marketing are well aligned with product and technology.

A culture of strong teamwork and collaboration is best suited to the matrix; it requires all parties to understand the big picture priorities and work to develop strategies and plans at the points they intersect.

A culture that is too control-centric will be challenged by operating a healthy matrix organisation. This is why the shift to a matrix structure as a business grows is one of the most challenging culture change programs faced.

There will be debate about what money and activity is held in each side of the matrix. Ultimately you need leaders who care about the company first and are good collaborators to land on the right approach.

If you think operating the matrix is a problem for your organisation, you are probably thinking too low in the order of things. There is probably a bigger issue of poor planning and alignment of expectations or a culture that is too control-centric and not collaborative enough. This problem usually presents in a senior person or people in the organisation who are not natural collaborators and don't want to let go of control.

The matrix works only as well as the culture of the people in it and the quality of their leadership.

Technology and the business

The ninemsn CEO role was my first as an organisation leader using technology to provide a service. Up to that point my experience was in selling technology to others who provided a service to their customers. The experience at ninemsn changed my thinking and mode of engagement with customers when I returned to the IT industry at Microsoft almost five years later.

The negative sentiments directed at technology by those who were users always troubled me. It seemed then, and still does now, acceptable for IT to be blamed for many of the difficulties organisations face in getting value from implementing new technology. But is it really technology that is the problem, or the user? Often the same technology successfully deployed in one environment is a disaster when implemented elsewhere.

I am not stupid or brave enough to defend the information technology industry against claims of overhype and creating complexity. However, my experience at ninemsn made me realise that many of the problems of IT implementation are due to a lack of alignment and poor change management.

In the early days at ninemsn, the IT team was a mess. The situation reflected the business in its early stages, trying to do too much. IT was blamed for many of the problems of the business at that time.

At first, I left it to our IT people to get it sorted out, but I soon discovered that the problem was like the home page development issues I described earlier, where lack of clarity and overall priority led to misalignment of IT with the needs of the business. I had to intervene as CEO and dig us out of that hole.

We added IT to the agenda of the executive team meetings and invested the time to understand the software development backlog. We then had to make the hard choices about what was and was not going to get resourced.

To this day, I remain astounded at how few organisations bring the IT priorities to the top team for collective review and prioritisation. Even companies in the software business often avoid or brush over this.

As ninemsn developed clarity of purpose and priorities and aligned around them, the challenge of making trade-offs between competing IT development and budget needs lessened. It became easier to choose between what had to be done and what would be nice to do or could be left for later.

The most important by-product of the prioritisation process was that we were able to communicate the rationale for the choices we made in the context of overall business priorities. Those who missed out on resourcing or funding were never happy but understood why. We also made sure to reset the objectives of those who missed out on resources so expectations of them were aligned with our ability to invest in the IT capabilities they needed.

> *Organisations that have consistent issues with IT exhibit a very strong sign that they are not aligned or well led. If your IT department or product development team is consistently not delivering, it's a leadership issue — blame your CEO.*

Short-term and long-term expectations

I love this saying: 'The best way to have a great long term is to have an ongoing series of great short terms.' Business commentators often refer to the quarterly reporting cycle of business as a reason why businesses and CEOs are short term in their thinking. Presumably this leads CEOs to avoid taking short-term steps to position their organisation for long-term, sustainable success. This view is simplistic. If short-term expectations or goals are not consistent with what is needed for long-term success, there must be misalignment. The following misalignments probably exist:

1. Current financial results (and expectations) rely too much on 'bad' or declining revenue and profit sources that are misaligned with the future prospects and longer-term health of the business. Bad revenue typically comes from billing or revenue management practices that exploit a customer's dependence on you. They help you in the short term but hurt customer relationships and the business longer term. Examples are telco

roaming charges and bank charges for use of ATMs — both of which have been significantly reduced in recent times.

2. Leadership culture and incentives are misaligned with what is good for the business in the longer term. This probably happens less than folklore suggests, but some executive teams will do what is in their short-term compensation interests rather than what is right for the business longer term. The move away from commissioned advisors in financial services is an example where action is being taken to better align short-term business activity with longer-term stakeholder success.

3. Investor expectations are not aligned with a full and proper understanding of the long-term prospects of the business.

4. Change has taken place in the operating environment — for example, a pandemic or shift in the economy that has rendered existing plans unsuitable.

It takes strong leadership and courage to overcome these alignment issues. A responsible approach is to confront these misalignments and surface the uncomfortable realities that require immediate action.

Confronting misalignment and resetting expectations with the financial markets and other stakeholders is a fundamental responsibility of Boards and CEOs, so the activities of the day align as best as possible with what's right for the longer term.

A great example of confronting these issues was the courage shown by Andy Penn, the CEO of Telstra, when I served on the Board of Telstra. Andy led us and ultimately all stakeholders on the journey of recognising that the practice of paying a 31-cent dividend at the time (typically 100 per cent of Telstra's profits) was unsustainable.

While Andy and the Board were heavily criticised, fundamental shifts in the industry, including the National Broadband Network and the potential entry of a fourth mobile carrier, meant that Telstra's longer-term financial health required a serious realignment of stakeholder expectations with reality.

Telstra could have found ways to keep paying a higher dividend for a few more years, but this would have harmed the business in the longer term. Andy, with support from the Board, stepped up to review Telstra's Capital Management policy and in doing so confront reality and redefine what success looked like.

It was not a popular move, and the Telstra share price was smashed (down 12 per cent) on announcement of the new dividend policy. There was no short-term benefit in taking these steps; however, to avoid the issue would have created ongoing misalignment of reality and expectation going forward.

During my five years as Xero CEO, we benefited from strong alignment with our shareholders and investors. We were very transparent about our intentions to invest for long-term growth. When post-pandemic increases to interest rates changed the way we and other growth businesses were valued, the pressure on us increased significantly to change our approach to one that was more balanced towards continued growth and better operating margins.

The need to reduce our expense structure became a dominant theme overnight and led to the difficult actions taken to reset the short-term investment settings of the business.

Final words on alignment

Alignment is the often missing and vital link to executing a strategy, leading change and great teams. Alignment demands difficult conversations and hard choices.

Alignment is a journey not an end state. The process is continuous and a function that reflects what is learned through a consistent review of performance. We discuss Performance Focus in the next chapter.

Chapter summary

Alignment is vital and often a missing or weakest link in execution and performance.

Questions to ask yourself (or to ask others about you):

- How would I score (out of 10) on how well aligned our team is to execute our strategy?

- Are the actions to execute our strategy aligned with the individual objectives of our people?

- Does our organisation work well across functions to execute our strategy?

- Do I have strong collaboration across the functions that deliver our products and services?

- Are my short-term objectives aligned with long-term success?

Recommended actions:

- Implement level order planning.

- Bring technology prioritisation decisions to the top team meetings of your organisation until expectations are clear.

- Confront and resolve issues causing short-term misalignment with long-term success or expectations.

Refer to the Must-Do Toolbox:

- Implement level order planning.

- Align to be a better product business.

CHAPTER 10

MUST-DO #6: FOCUS ON PERFORMANCE

Clarity and alignment evolve from a focus on performance by having the right conversations with the right people at the right time about the progress of important strategic initiatives and work programs.

The devil is in the detail

When I was appointed Managing Director of Microsoft Australia and New Zealand, I joined my predecessor, Paul Houghton, on a visit to Microsoft's headquarters for the annual 'mid-year review' (MYR) meeting, which was quite a ritual.

At MYR, each subsidiary leader was subjected to a detailed examination of their business performance. The review process was pretty much a business version of having a colonoscopy, something you didn't look forward to.

I sat next to Paul on the flight to the United States, going over the 'MYR Presentation Deck', which included reams of text and data presented in Excel spreadsheets covering every aspect of business operations. Details of performance by market segment, product, channel and every other dimension were included. Of immediate concern to me was the size of the font on the MYR spreadsheet. It was so small I couldn't read it! Fortunately, with a stronger prescription of reading glasses, I adapted.

The MYR meeting was arranged using a large u-shaped seating plan where the subsidiary management team occupied one side of the table, surrounded by an audience of typically 50 or more executives from most functions of corporate headquarters. The meeting went for half to a full day, depending on the size and relative importance of the subsidiary to the overall Microsoft business.

The roots of MYR evolved under Bill Gates' leadership of Microsoft and carried into the Steve Ballmer era. There were legends about people who did not survive MYR because they didn't know the answer to a question Bill might ask. According to one of these legends, Bill was unhappy with the response to a question he asked a country manager and followed up by asking which college they had graduated from. On hearing the answer, he turned to the head of human resources and said they should remind him never to hire people from that college!

The MYR presentation document contained enough background information to ensure that if you were asked any question about anything, you would have the answer. I lived through five years of mid-year review as a subsidiary leader and never enjoyed it, but I couldn't deny the value of drilling into the detail of performance.

MYR was also a great forum to communicate the customer and competitive issues we were confronting in our market. The issues raised were noted and managed through to a response or some feedback on how the company intended to address it.

One downside of MYR was that corporate executives running the process occasionally used the forum as a place to grandstand and embarrass the subsidiary management team under review. It was always great to get through the MYR alive and unscathed, and completion of the meeting was followed by some serious celebration.

MYR was an effective process to help assess the quality of the leaders of each subsidiary and to determine if they were executing to plan.

It was also a great vehicle for bringing the subsidiary management teams together to review and prepare for the corporate review of business performance.

If your performance management systems don't drill into the detail, you are not applying adequate diligence or testing to ensure that clarity and alignment exist to execute your strategy.

An effective rhythm of the business

The 'rhythm of the business' (ROB) is the regular cadence of meetings that keep an organisation or team clear, aligned and focused on performance. The discipline of holding the right meetings at the right time to review performance against strategic objectives is essential. The nature of the rhythm can vary depending on the size and maturity of an organisation.

I often hear people complain about the time they spend in meetings, which reflects the low value of the meetings they attend.

I believe strongly that until an organisation or team can say they are clear, aligned and performing well, they need meetings and plenty of them; however, the agenda must be right and the difficult conversations and hard choices must be had. Many organisations I've advised have not had an established or adequate ROB for the strategic change they were initiating or responding to.

Meetings should take place at least once a month for any team to discuss strategic priorities, actions and performance against objectives. In large organisations, each division or functional senior management team should be meeting monthly. Weekly one-hour 'update' meetings and short 'stand-up' meetings are acceptable but are not a substitute for detailed discussion of key strategic objectives, particularly those not performing to expectation.

Organisations with team members dispersed around the world should meet face-to-face for two or three days, up to three times a year if possible. Communicating using Hangout, Skype or Zoom is common practice and convenient, but it doesn't replace the benefit of spending time together in person as a team. The difficult conversations regarding progress of executing strategic priorities and actions are more effective and productive if people are in the room together.

At Xero, the ROB meeting cadence evolved each year as the business grew and conditions changed. During the pandemic we increased the frequency of meetings as we adjusted our budget settings in response to our assessment of changing business conditions. The meetings I found most valuable were:

- weekly sales performance update — chaired by our Chief Customer Officer, for 30 minutes every Friday morning on the sales performance of the week. The Top 60 leaders across the business were invited to dial in to this virtual meeting.

- weekly leadership team meetings — with a rotating Chair and the agenda set by our Head of Operations

- quarterly business review — with the Top 60 leaders, to review progress in executing our strategic priorities

- people leader meetings — held three times a year to update our people leaders on the state of the business, and to focus on the development of a specific area of skill, such as career planning and development.

To make sure the ROB your team employs is the right one, have a conversation with your team that specifically asks these questions:

- Are our meetings productive and of good quality?

- Are they held at the right time and with the right agenda?

- If not, when should we meet and what agendas should we set for our meetings?

If possible, these conversations are best when facilitated by an objective third party in a safe environment.

The right scorecard

If the alignment process and level order planning are conducted as described in the previous chapter, the top strategic priorities and actions for an organisation will be defined clearly and have sensible key performance indicators (KPIs) attached to measure progress.

KPIs are not always popular in business folklore because they are often blamed for driving the wrong outcomes or behaviours. I don't subscribe to this view that the KPI is to blame. Usually it reflects an unreasonable target for the KPI, rather than the KPI itself.

As mentioned earlier, the metrics associated with executing strategy will be a combination of soft metrics (leading indicators of health) and hard metrics (indicators of past performance).

Soft metrics are those aligned with the human and relationship aspects of organisation or team performance, such as Net Promoter Score (NPS) for customer satisfaction, or an engagement score for employee satisfaction. They can also include leading indicators to track whether strategic actions are creating the outcomes for future success (for example, adding the desired number of new distributors to your sales channels).

Hard metrics are those that reflect the financial and physical elements of business performance, such as revenue, profit, cash generation and inventory. These metrics tell you a lot about what has happened, but don't always provide insight to future progress or the quality of current execution.

A blend of the two metrics is important. The right soft metrics are as valuable as any other metrics if they are aligned with the execution of strategy.

An issue with survey-based soft metrics like NPS is that they are often sourced through intervention in the customer experience (tampering with the sample) and their inclusion in compensation calculations can lead to manipulation. As data analytics improve and customer journeys and experiences are increasingly analysed without asking customers individually, soft metrics will provide even more relevant insights into performance.

The final thing to keep in mind with scorecards is to focus on and measure the few objectives and metrics that matter most.

Establishing the right scorecard at Xero created an important foundation to improving our digital sales and marketing performance. After visiting Adobe we realised we did not have an adequate process and discipline to track our performance from top of funnel through to conversion to sale. Our Chief Customer Officer, Rachael Powell, and her team established a tracking and review process called JEDI, which changed the nature of our conversations and discipline in this important part of the business.

It's good to remember that people respect what you inspect.

People manager performance

Employee engagement surveys and feedback on management performance are important soft metrics, but they must overcome the following shortfalls or traps:

- **Trap #1: 'We have an employee opinion survey, but nothing ever comes of it.'** This situation is not good for the credibility of leadership. Managers must review the results with their team members and work to address the issues. Not all issues can be easily or quickly fixed, and if that's the case it helps to explain the rationale for a slow or delayed fix so people understand and feel heard.

- **Trap #2: 'We have an employee opinion survey. However, we're not sure the results are accurate because people can be "influenced" by their boss to give a good score.'** Dealing with this issue is a serious question of leadership from the top.

Attempts to use threats or inducements of any kind to distort responses to a survey are unacceptable and destructive to the culture of the organisation.

Survey integrity depends on a genuine desire to ensure that if results are not good, the manager concerned is helped to improve their performance, rather than reprimanded for the result.

- **Trap #3: 'We have an employee survey, but we keep score only at the departmental level, rather than the individual manager level.'** This is a cop-out! Anyone who manages people must get feedback.

Sometimes I hear that feedback surveys for managers with fewer than five people should be avoided in order to protect their team members' confidentiality. That confidentiality only matters if the manager's performance is an issue. The dilemma here is that you eliminate one way of surfacing those issues. In this case, other mechanisms like 'skip interviews' should be used to find out how the people leader is performing.

While we are on this subject, why have managers with four or fewer reports? Sometimes it's unavoidable, but wherever possible, small management spans should be avoided, so a people leader can focus on leading their team rather than being in a hybrid role also as an individual contributor.

Individual performance management

There are different schools of thought regarding the merit of individual performance reviews. Whatever the sentiment about their form and nature, there should be regular reviews by managers of their people. If people are not performing to their potential, it is essential to understand why and help them improve.

Performance management and confronting poor performance are tough, and so they should be. I don't buy complaints about how hard Industrial Relations or other regulations make it to ask someone to leave the business. These complaints are largely myth, given that there are very few cases of unfair dismissal in the courts at any time, relative to the millions of people employed.

> *The starting position with any performance issue should be that the organisation is failing when an employee is not performing to their potential or to a standard consistent with what is expected. Remember, you hired them!*

I remember how nervous I was as a first-time manager giving corrective feedback. I didn't sleep much the night before the meeting and leant heavily on my notes and advice prepared with my rep from the HR department.

We are human, we want to be liked, so it's understandable that we fear and sometimes avoid confronting poor-performing team members. But no matter how painful, we must step up because avoidance seriously impacts our credibility with other team members. Avoidance is deeply damaging to the person concerned if it means they lose time and the opportunity to find a role they might be better suited to.

The high performers know who the poor performers are

Good performers have a reasonable expectation that management will deal directly with poor performance. There should be no excuses, but in practice there are many. Here are some common excuses I have seen play out:

- *'Having this person in the role is better than having no one.'* Perhaps the most damaging aspect of this excuse is the belief that a poor performer is better than having no one in the position. This overlooks the negative impact a poor-performing team member has on others around them. Every day a poor performer remains in the job is another day before a suitable, better replacement can be found.

- *'Headcount or budget is tight, so I may not get a replacement for the staff member if I manage them out of the business.'*

A manager using this excuse to avoid confronting a poor performer lacks support from management up the line to do the right thing. There should be no such disincentive to avoid stepping up to deal with poor performance.

- *'I think it's time for this person to move to another department.'* Playing 'pass the parcel' with underachievers shifts the problem from one manager to another and ultimately delays the opportunity to confront the performance problem. Managers who move poor performers as a way of avoiding confrontation of performance issues should get a serious talking to.

- *'This person's performance may improve.'* This approach makes sense if the performance management process is underway and clear direction is provided on the improvements that need to be made.

- *'I'm too busy to deal with the problem,'* or *'It won't be long before I move to another management position.'* I don't need to explain why this is indefensible.

All these excuses and consequences of not honestly and directly confronting individual performance issues create financial and spiritual pain. The financial impacts include the negative influence on the productivity of other team members and the organisation not performing to its potential. The spiritual impact includes loss of management credibility and the resulting impact on morale. This can lead to the most damaging consequence of all — the loss of good people.

Stepping up to confronting people and performance issues is important to realising the aspirations of the organisation and creating a great team environment.

> The Must-Do Toolbox in Part IV contains a detailed guide on how to best confront individual performance issues.

Team performance focus

It has often surprised and concerned me that the measurement and management of team performance is not pursued with the importance it deserves. Beyond the character of the CEO or team leader, there is nothing more important to executing strategic change initiatives than how the leadership team functions, and how teams across the organisation perform.

Following is a simple diagnostic tool that can help provide insight and tangible measurement of the performance of a team.

Team performance to potential diagnostic

This tool is a great way to get focus on becoming a better team, team leader or team member.

Step 1: Diagnose

Ask team members to individually score, on a scale of 0 to 10 (with 10 being the highest score and 0 the lowest score), their answer to the following question:

With the resources we have available today, how is our team (or leadership group) performing relative to what is possible?

The references to 'resources we have available today' is important because this exercise aims to form an assessment of existing potential, rather than potential that is subject to the availability of more money or human resources.

The scoring process is best done anonymously, especially if the leader of the team is present. I don't care how receptive they are to feedback, people are *never* as frank as they should be in an open forum when their boss is present.

Once each team member has submitted their score, they should be collated and the high score, low score and the average score revealed. The average matters most, but it's good to know the range of answers.

I have run this simple test in many forums and discovered that the average score for most teams or groups is between 5 and 6.5 out of 10. Most teams have some work to do to achieve their potential. Any score above 7 (good) or 8 (excellent) indicates a very good team or group at work. Good organisations I have surveyed are often very self-critical, rating themselves around 6 to 7.

Sadly, fewer than half the people I have surveyed have *ever* worked on a team that scored 8 or higher out of 10.

Step 2: Discuss

Ask each person in the team what they think is the *one thing* they would change in order to improve team performance for the better. The fascinating thing about this step is that 9 out of 10 things people suggest have nothing to do with the industry their organisation is in.

The issues are generic to most organisations and relate to matters like how people work together, lack of prioritisation, bad resource allocation, or poor behaviours and culture. These are all in the control of the group to fix without much excuse, if the team leader is supportive.

Step 3: Act

Once each person is heard, the group should discuss and agree (or vote if needed) on the one thing the team is committed to improving. Identify a leader and supporters of that change process and follow up at the next team meeting to check on progress.

The benefit of this exercise is that it gets the teams focused on and regularly discussing opportunities to improve performance.

When measuring team performance, keep the process of diagnosis as simple as possible and pick just one or two of the lowest scoring areas for improvement (no more). Then get serious about fixing the most pressing problem.

For boards and senior management, it's important to remember that turning team performance measurement into metrics, such as those generated by a regular team diagnostic, is a very useful way to monitor and gain insight into an important leading indicator of success and failure: the quality of leadership and teamwork in the organisation.

Final words on performance focus

Holding regular and thorough performance reviews underpins the ability to adapt and learn from experience, and to raise the quality of performance at an organisation, team and individual level. The better the process, the faster a change journey and team will navigate towards the desired destination.

If you want your change program to succeed and your team to achieve its potential, make sure your organisation or team have the right scorecard and meetings, and the necessary focus on performance at business, manager, individual and team level.

Chapter summary

- The devil is in the detail of performance. If you are not on track you need to review and adjust where you are heading (clarity) and/or how you are executing (alignment).

- Focus on team performance, not just business and individual performance.

Questions to ask yourself (or to ask others about you):

- Does my team focus on the detail of business performance?

- Do I have the right meetings and scorecard to measure progress executing strategic initiatives?

- Do I have the right focus on the performance of our people managers, their teams and their direct reports?

Recommended actions:

- Establish an effective rhythm of the business, with the right scorecard.

- Measure people manager performance and don't accept poor performance.

- Establish diagnostic and measurement processes to assess and improve team performance.

- Run the Must-Do Diagnostic in chapter 13.

Refer to the Must-Do Toolbox:

- Confront individual performance issues.

CHAPTER 11

MUST-DO #7: HAVE DIFFICULT CONVERSATIONS

The speed of change is a function of our ability to speak about the need for change in honest and direct terms. The spoken and written word is all we have. The faster the world changes, the more we need to confront difficult conversations and make hard choices.

We must get more comfortable being uncomfortable.

Words are all we have

People who run start-up businesses are rarely comfortable. They operate day to day knowing that their future is not assured. People who run established businesses need to think the same way. To evolve with the change they seek or are responding to, they need to be willing to try new things, take chances and be prepared to fail.

Andy Grove, former CEO of Intel, famously said, 'Only the paranoid survive', to emphasise the importance of treating the threats of change seriously, and dealing with them as if they are real.

How we talk reflects how we think. If our talk isn't honest and direct, it is fair to expect that our thinking may be complacent or fearful. And when organisations allow 'sacred cows' or 'un-discussable' subjects to get in the way of change, the consequences can be severe.

It is critical to have the difficult conversations about the following questions:

1. Is what we do still relevant?

Leaders need to question their organisation or team's purpose, and why it exists, rather than be ruled by it.

Some of the most difficult conversations I was party to at Xero revolved around what we wanted to be and should not be. The conversations led us to change our purpose to: 'To be the most trusted and insightful small business platform'. The conversations around potential acquisitions and how they might support or distract us from our purpose were also difficult because we had to coalesce a range of conflicting views to land on a clear position.

2. Are we adequately focused?

No business has unlimited resources available to it. Another fertile domain of difficult conversations is talking about what you can do and won't do with the resources or investment envelope available. These conversations include debates over the technology and development backlog, where doing too much can seriously impact project timelines, quality and success.

At Xero, we had a very capable strategy and corporate development team looking at emerging cloud accounting and software businesses around the world. The team put together a good argument that we should look at an acquisition in Europe. The business concerned was small, fast-growing and well led. On the negative side, the technology overlapped our existing stack, and the valuation commanded was very high.

Everyone on the management team was keen to pursue it except our CTO, Mark Rees, for good reason. The Board was prepared to support the acquisition largely because of management's conviction, and they looked to me to make the call.

Throughout the process, I had a nagging concern that while the acquisition had great merit, it presented a significant distraction from our core priorities at the time.

As pressure mounted to make the final go-ahead call, I gathered the people who had worked together on the process and explained that I couldn't agree to proceed. The people involved were disappointed but respected the decision and the time I took to explain the rationale to them.

Saying no to good ideas is an essential aspect of staying focused and executing well. While it is difficult to do, saying no to good ideas stops people trying to do too many things without the resources they need to really succeed. While painful, it is the kindest act.

3. How is our business performing?

Before IBM ran into serious trouble in the early nineties, it lacked honest and direct talk about performance. For example, it was forbidden for salespeople to blame a product deficiency for the loss of a sale. More acceptable reasons for losing the business were failure to build a relationship with the customer, or failure to sell the value of our offering. This served to protect the product development groups (where power ultimately lay at that time) from market reality for way too long.

If a product or process is bad, acknowledge it as soon as possible and avoid excuses and defensive behaviour that stifles straight talk.

I worked with a start-up that was building a product in the employee engagement measurement space. At one of our Board meetings, it was clear from the online traffic measurement data that user engagement with the product was poor. When questioned about the issue, the management team started making excuses for the decline in engagement, highlighting seasonality and a couple of other potential excuses.

I stopped the conversations and made it clear that we had to face reality and call the performance what it was. Bad! Unless we did that, we wouldn't treat the need for remediation with the intensity required to make progress.

Covering up or dressing up reasons for poor performance is costly and dangerous.

4. Are our people performing well?

Changing an organisation means changing people. Some will make it, some won't. Failure to confront people performance issues undermines change and the credibility of organisation leaders. You also risk losing good performers who know who the poor performers are.

Legendary NFL Coach Bill Parcells transformed several poor-performing teams into winning teams. He said, 'You have to be honest with people — brutally honest. You have to tell them the truth about their performance, you have to tell it to them face-to-face…Sometimes the truth will be painful, and sometimes saying it will lead to an uncomfortable confrontation. So be it.'

I strongly believe you can be brutally honest and show empathy if you take the time.

When I was 18 and a university student working on the driveway of a suburban liquor store, my boss, Joe, asked me to mop the floor.

I was busy at it when he tapped me on the shoulder and said, 'Steve, you're a good bloke, but you have no idea how to mop a floor. Let me show you how.'

He took the mop from my hands and showed me his well-seasoned technique, which involved a more productive approach to ringing out the mop and covering the floor. He returned the mop to me with a friendly pat on the back and said, 'Away you go, son.'

I appreciated the way he turned my poor performance into a learning experience and that he showed real care towards me.

Honest and direct feedback is fundamental to high performance at work, and changing times demand that those conversations happen much more frequently.

The key ingredients to confronting difficult conversations are context, care and courage.

Clear context

You can't have an effective conversation about a performance issue if you don't provide a clear context for why a concern exists. You must set clear objectives for the business and people so they understand what is important and what is expected.

People who do not 'fit in' to an organisation often move on at their own initiative once they have clarity of expectations and recognise that there isn't alignment with their personal interest, skills and desires.

Clear context provides people with a real understanding of where the organisation is heading and what is expected.

Care

When conducting difficult conversations you should 'play the ball, not the person'. You can say the hardest things in a humane way, if you care and take the time. There is no need to be abusive in a difficult conversation.

Staying calm, objective and grounded in a clear business context can preserve relationships when you're confronting some of the toughest issues. Caring about people and showing respect for them, even if it requires them to leave the business, is an important way to keep the social network of your business strong.

Courage

It can be stressful and scary to overcome the fear of having difficult conversations. But with experience, confronting and working through issues allows you to gain confidence and to see the benefit for all concerned. This in turn will reduce the level of fear experienced when you step up to the next challenge.

> The Must-Do Toolbox in Part IV has a detailed guide on how to confront and address individual performance issues.

Confront difficult conversations about performance

Asking the Human Resources department to handle issues with a poor-performing team member is abdicating responsibility from where it lies — with the people manager. It's fine to seek advice and support from HR because building management capability is part of their role; however, it is the manager's job to step up and confront the issue.

My ability to deal with poor performance improved greatly when I adopted a mindset that reduced the 'emotional' pressure I felt in dealing with people performance issues.

> *This mindset is based on being a facilitator between the organisation and individual's needs and showing genuine care and desire to help the person concerned.*

This requires a genuine interest in helping the person concerned to understand the performance issues and to improve, and a genuine desire to see the situation turn around.

Poor performance is never entirely the employee's fault. The organisation bears responsibility because it hired the employee. The company is also more culpable if the team member has had performance concerns for some time without being appropriately confronted with the issues.

The problem can also be that the nature of the role and associated needs have changed. I've heard this issue framed by the expression that the person was a round peg in a round hole, but then the hole turned square. They might have been a good fit for their role in the past, but needs have changed so the role has changed. It's their current fit for the role that is causing concern.

The approach I have learned is to be supportive rather than confrontational; to step back to become a facilitator between the company's needs and the employee's needs, capability and performance.

Position yourself as a moderator or facilitator between the company and the team member, demonstrating care for the needs of both. This approach reduces the chance that the employee feels under personal attack; rather, they sense genuine concern for their wellbeing, as well as understanding what's right for the business.

This approach only works if you are authentic and genuinely care about the person. You can't fake it.

I have often stepped up and dealt with performance issues and found that over time the people impacted appreciated the honesty and support that came with confronting the issue.

For the most part, even those ultimately managed out of the organisation end up thanking you for the change and opportunities that followed, once they moved on from the role they were not well suited to.

Not everyone will find your negative assessment of their performance reasonable, so there will be some who won't have good things to say about you. Unfortunately, in these circumstances, the difficult conversations have relationship fallout that can't be avoided. It's a 'bad vs badder' situation that people leaders must confront from time to time.

Bullying claims

If an organisation has not had a culture of performance feedback and management and decides to implement one, the immediate and almost inevitable fallout will be claims of bullying by people receiving tough feedback.

It's important not to let these claims stop the process, but to persist and make sure that the approach being taken is fair and respectful towards the person impacted. Bullying is unacceptable; however, it should never be confused with carefully considered and delivered performance feedback, even if it is hard for the receiver to hear or accept.

The master

The first time I saw Steve Jobs in action was in his role as an advisor to then Apple CEO Gil Amelio. I was Vice President, Apple Asia Pacific, and had been invited to observe a meeting with Gil and the Apple executive team reviewing several new initiatives with Steve Jobs and Steve Wozniak present.

The marketing team had just presented a new Apple advertising campaign planned for *The Wall Street Journal*, which claimed, 'We're back … with great new products'.

As the marketing executive leading the presentation wrapped up the session, he thanked his team for their great work. Steve, who had been silent to that point in the presentation, raised his hand asking Gil if he could speak. He asked the executive, 'When you thanked the team just then for their great work, did you mean great work compared to what Apple has done in recent times, or did you mean great relative to the work Nike is doing?'

Nike at the time was firing on all cylinders as one of the world's best marketing companies.

The executive replied, 'I meant great work relative to Apple's more recent efforts.'

'That's good, because their work might be great relative to what Apple has recently produced, but it's important that the team understands that relative to what Nike is doing, it is shit.'

Steve continued, 'By the way, you are putting a full-page ad in *The Wall Street Journal* which says "We're back" when every second page in *The Wall Street Journal* says we are dead. Does that really make sense?'

Suffice to say, the full page with 'We're back' didn't see the light of day when the campaign launched.

There's no executive I ever watched who talked more directly than Steve Jobs. At times he was unnecessarily harsh, but in making tough calls he was impressive.

The first time I felt that something special might happen under Steve's new leadership of Apple was during an executive offsite at Pajaro Dunes beach retreat in California in 1997, with about a hundred Apple executives from around the world present. As with all my Steve Jobs encounters, it was extremely memorable.

After dinner, as we mingled for drinks, I found myself face to face with Steve and suggested he should visit Australia sometime in the near future.

He just looked at me with a half blank expression on his face and said, 'Why the fuck would I want to go to Australia?'

At the time I was a bit offended and told Steve to forget I asked. However, on reflection I realised that visiting Australia was way out of his focus at the time. To be fair, it was not a great suggestion given the challenges Steve was trying to navigate Apple through at the time.

At the Pajaro Dunes retreat Steve introduced the new Apple strategy he described as 'Swatch', after the watch company — affordable, friendly, elegant and ultimately disposable technology. Steve and design guru Jonathan Ive unveiled the new, soon to be released (in many colours) iMac prototype.

After the presentation was over, Steve and Jonathan continued to collaborate. Hunched over the prototype, they discussed the shape and form of the computer that would ultimately be the first in a long line of home runs that Steve would hit in his second life at Apple.

For the first time in my experience at Apple, clarity and alignment started to emerge from the leader.

Practise giving feedback

Feedback 'speed dating' is a great exercise for teams to practise having conversations that help improve how they engage with each other. I encourage this exercise on a regular basis to help build great teams.

> The Must-Do Toolbox has a guide outlining the easy steps to make this part of your change and team journey.

Final word on having difficult conversations

Words are all we have, and the quality of the words we speak defines how quickly clarity emerges, alignment challenges are confronted and performance is honestly assessed. From there, move as quickly as possible to improve and adjust course.

Having difficult conversations is central to an effective change journey and developing and maintaining a great team. Difficult conversations are also a precursor to making hard choices, with the quality of those conversations often shaping the quality of the choices.

In the next chapter, we look at the last of the Must-Dos: Make Hard Choices.

Chapter summary

Getting clear and aligned, and reviewing performance honestly, depends on the speed and quality of difficult conversations. There is a kind way to say hard things if you care and take the time.

Questions to ask yourself (or to ask others about you):

- Am I actively confronting the most important strategic questions and the biggest operational performance issues?
- Do I confront the difficult conversations or avoid them?
- Do I give feedback in a constructive way?
- What could I do better to help have the difficult conversations?

Recommended actions:

- Encourage difficult conversations by asking the following questions:
  - Why are we doing what we do, and is it still relevant?
  - What are our priorities and are we adequately focused?
  - How is our business really performing?
  - Which of our people are not performing to expectation?
- Approach difficult conversations with context, care for people impacted, and courage.
- Practise and encourage giving feedback.
- Run training for team members on how to have difficult conversations.

(continued)

Refer to the Must-Do Toolbox:

- Confront individual performance issues.
- Practise feedback speed dating.

CHAPTER 12

MUST-DO #8: MAKE HARD CHOICES

Many years ago I was fortunate to hear American author John Stoessinger speak about leadership. Stoessinger witnessed President John F Kennedy's cabinet deliberate over the US response to the Cuban Missile Crisis of 1962. Stoessinger described leadership as 'making the choice between bad and badder', and it's an expression that has stuck with me.

Prioritising our time

We face this reality in work and life when we are forced to prioritise, say, between career and family time, or between living where you are and moving overseas. The same applies broadly to prioritising our time. If you don't make hard choices, you suffer from doing too much. If you do make the hard choice, you may miss out on something big or something you could have done with success, which is why clarity of purpose and ambition is so important. The clearer you are, the better you can prioritise the things that matter most. Prioritisation is a big test for all of us.

At ninemsn we had a hard choice to make about whether we would build an education portal alongside our core consumer business. Great people in the business were strongly advocating for us to do it. After many discussions and detailed scoping work, we decided not to pursue it.

I remember feeling bad about the decision because some team members were disappointed, and the education market could have been a big, missed opportunity. In hindsight, though, it was the right decision and allowed us to focus on the core consumer business. In time, the education market evolved very differently from what we had anticipated; ninemsn was built to serve consumers, and staying committed to that purpose was a good call.

Making hard choices will not make everyone around you happy. That's what makes them hard. When making hard choices ensure the following:

- The right people have been involved and feel heard.

- Those who are disappointed feel respected and understand why the decision did not go their way.

- The basis of the choice — pros and cons — has been carefully thought through against a clear higher purpose or big-picture context.

- The person charged with making the final decision is trusted and in service of others, demonstrating care for those impacted by the decision.

Hard choices often involve short-term pain to achieve long-term gain. In my experience the short-term pain is usually worth it to get to a better place. Unfortunately, that doesn't make it easier for people (like me) who must deal with the short-term pain.

Throughout my career I have observed or been party to many hard choices including major career decisions, choosing the right CEO, making across-the-board job cuts or replacing the founder of a business.

Hiring the right CEO

I served for nine years on the Board of Telstra, Australia's largest telecommunications company. Geoff Cousins, a very successful former executive in the media, advertising and cable TV industry, served with me in the early years of my Board tenure. His words to me, in his gravelly voice, still ring in my ears today: 'The one thing a Board does that really matters is to hire the right CEO.'

Geoff is right. I've aways felt that the life of a Board Director is great, even in tough times, if your CEO and Chair are of good character and capability. If one of the two is not, being a Board Director is a worrying and challenging experience. If both are not, being a Board Director is a nightmare to be avoided.

That said, Geoff's advice poses the question, how do you know if you are hiring the right CEO? Well, unfortunately you can't be 100 per cent sure until well after you hire them. The risk is generally lower if you hire internally and have good insight into the character and capability of the candidate.

Recruiting an external candidate is a riskier proposition. Interviews and presentations during the recruitment process are no guarantee for ensuring the character and capability you are getting. Reference checking can be flawed because referees provided by the candidate are going to be favourable.

Where referees are not provided by the candidate, you might be lucky enough to dodge a bullet because someone you stumble across alerts you to serious concerns. Most referees, however, will be more polite than they should.

The initial response from referees to the question of how they describe working with the candidate is an important one to gauge. If the answer is functional, rather than emotional, you should dig deeper. What you want to hear first is how much they loved working with the candidate, rather than a functional answer such as the candidate is smart and hard working.

Referees can't really provide you with detailed insight into whether the candidate is going to work well in your environment. The character of a CEO has such influence over the nature of an organisation that in addition to answering the question, *Which person do we want our next CEO to be?* the question that really needs answering is, *Which person do we want our organisation to be?*

When comparing a candidate of high character and lower experience with a candidate of untested or unknown character with greater experience, it makes sense to weight the *character* gap at a meaningful premium to the *experience* gap when selecting between the two.

That said, what makes this process among the hardest choices is the uncertainty that will exist until some time after the decision is made.

Another related choice is to decide the length of the transition from the outgoing CEO to the new CEO, and whether the outgoing CEO should remain involved in the business on the Board or in some other capacity. Clearly, the decision will vary depending on the circumstances around the transition. It's preferable to have a short transition with the previous CEO no longer involved in the business to give the new CEO freedom to get going and be as frank as possible about how they see the business. At Xero, the transition from me to Sukhinder Singh Cassidy was swift and effective, allowing Sukhinder, a smart and energetic leader, to grab the steering wheel and start quickly shaping Xero for its next phase.

Replacing a founder

Replacing a founder is one of the hardest choices a Board and management team will confront. I was fortunate to follow Rod Drury, who recognised the point in time when his capabilities and desires no longer aligned with how he saw the needs of the business.

I couldn't have asked for a better partnership than the one I had with Rod. From time to time we would disagree on things, but Rod always respected that as CEO, I had to make the call. A smooth founder transition is a big milestone for any business; the challenge is knowing when it's the right time and facing up to making the transition happen.

A friend of mine, who was an executive of a very successful founder-led technology company, shared with me that the founder was incredibly self-centred and no longer up to the task of running the business. He felt this way despite the business still growing revenue strongly and being one of the few people who had survived more than two years working for the founder. He told me that aside from one Board director, who was asking the right questions, most were generally hostages to the founder and did not challenge or dig too deep on issues of the founder's performance and impact on the people they led.

My friend believed the company was performing below its potential because it had outgrown the founder.

So the dilemma is this. Do you remove the founder from the CEO role and risk the short-term disruption, or not?

- First, the Board needs to know exactly what is going on in the business with the founder and the leadership team. It is important that a process is used to understand the team dynamic, such as those I outline in this book, and that fear among those providing feedback is managed carefully.

- Once the current state or reality is known, the Board can start their work of ensuring the founder gets the feedback needed and help to develop. The Board can also put in place a process to build internal and external succession depth.

- Following these actions, progress can be monitored and the chances of a smooth transition — as best as possible — can be contemplated.

So why do successful founders struggle to grow as leaders as their business scales? Initially, for those that succeed (most don't) their character and capability suit the early stages of the business like no one else could. They *are* the business. As the business grows, their direct impact starts to reduce and the need to work through others and have indirect impact increases. Working through others requires character and capabilities that are different and increasingly in demand as the business grows bigger.

Figure 12.1 (overleaf) shows the universe of two businesses, a start-up and a business that has scaled. The circle within the circle represents the importance of the founder's direct impact, while the white space shows the indirect impact.

As the business grows, the character and capability of the founder must change with it. For example, as a business scales, the founder must increasingly transition from Star Player to Head Coach. Not all founders are capable enough or motivated to adapt to that reality. Recognising when a founder has been outgrown and replacing them is a hard choice to make.

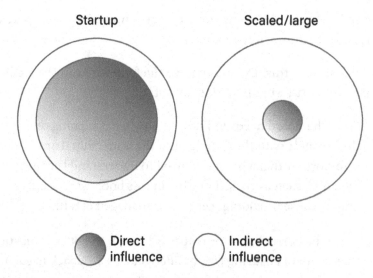

Startup   Scaled/large

Direct
influence

Indirect
influence

Figure 12.1: direct and indirect founder influence

Letting someone have their way (against your judgement)

Allowing people to have their way, even when you have a difference of opinion, is a hard choice to make for people leaders. Doing so can be a powerful sign of trust and care. Where the short-term risks are manageable, there are benefits in letting people have their way and allowing them to learn from mistakes (if they fail). You never know, they may be right and end up teaching you something.

In the early days at ninemsn, I had the authority to decide which television and magazine properties would have a website created, and which would not. I was under a lot of pressure from some of the group publishers at ACP to add their magazines to our already long list of sites in operation or in development.

Nick Chan, the group publisher responsible for the *Australian Women's Weekly*, was keen to accelerate the timeframe on the build of a website for the magazine. I wasn't at all enthusiastic about the idea, but Nick offered to fund it and take responsibility for generating revenue for the site, so I agreed. The conditions were that the site had to be built on ninemsn's network technology platforms and be consistent with our standards of navigation and design. The site was built and giving Nick his way led to a stronger relationship that served both of us well going forward.

Several months later, Nick and I caught up for a chat and he admitted to me that building, operating and selling the site was much harder than he had imagined. He said he now understood my reluctance to build it in the first place.

Making what you think is the right choice may not be right if the impact of your taking a stand leaves others feeling disempowered, or if their opportunity to learn and develop is lost.

Entering new markets and lines of business

I met with the Directors of an online sales and product distribution business that has achieved success in significant part due to the technology platform they developed in-house.

Management was keen to spin off the Technology Division and have it generate revenue by providing services to other businesses. In addition to potential financial benefits, the spin-off would help retain key members of the technology team who were passionate about pursuing this opportunity and looking for personal growth.

A new business opportunity like this looks attractive at the conceptual stage because you haven't confronted the reality of the complexity it creates. In this case you need to weigh up the benefits of additional revenue (and hopefully profit) and retaining a few key people, with several downside considerations:

- distraction of top management of the company from the current core business

- distraction of technology leadership from supporting the core business

- operational complexity caused by intercompany billing and service-level agreements.

I asked if the core business had growth potential and the answer was plenty. On that basis I suggested that unless the spin-off was going to be incredibly lucrative, I wouldn't do it owing to the downside considerations noted, and the likely benefits of staying focused on the core business.

Unfortunately, that would mean disappointing management and potentially losing some important technology talent.

Entering new markets and lines of business should always be treated as a hard choice. If it looks easy, you probably haven't adequately considered the downside risks. In my experience the upside is more likely to be overestimated and the downside risks underestimated.

Alternatively, moving into new markets and lines of business can be an imperative because current business growth prospects are limited, or the core business is so successful that the company has the financial resources and ability to acquire the talent to pursue new opportunities successfully. Apple, Microsoft, Google and Amazon are successfully demonstrating how this is done.

Whatever the situation, these new opportunities should be pursued only if you are able to do them with the right level of investment, with the right people and with dedicated focus. If all those considerations line up, the important thing left to get right is the management system that ensures new ventures are effectively governed with limited distraction to the current core business.

Making across-the-board job cuts

As the pandemic health emergency subsided during 2022, further uncertainty and challenges emerged with constraints in supply chains and limited availability of people to join the workforce. Rising inflation was met with a rapid increase in interest rates by central banks around the world, and with that emerged significant economic uncertainty and a radical shift in the expectations of investors.

Technology company valuations were re-rated with significant drops from the peaks of 2021. The dramatic change in the cost of money and the higher rate of return demanded of investment in new initiatives led many companies to make the hard choice to reduce their workforce and cut activities that extended beyond their core.

Much of this action was in response to the immediate shift in investor/owner expectations, with pressure on companies to show growth and profit, rather than the strong orientation towards investing for growth, when money was cheap.

While shareholders feel better as companies take these actions, they also need to be mindful that the associated increase in share price is potentially a short-term sugar hit. It is doubtful that any company that announced these cuts is immediately operationally better off than they were prior, unless their cuts are targeted and immediately improved focus by exiting discrete areas of activity.

Across-the-board cuts, announced as a substantial percentage of the total employee base, cost an organisation more than the restructuring charge and write-down in the valuation of assets under the new economic regime. Remember, most of the value of these companies is intangible, and the additional intangible costs of the cuts and restructures include:

- the short-term impact on productivity due to the disruption to existing ways of operating and the relationships that enable it

- a potential long-term impact on growth, noting that conversations about investing for growth and the future become relegated to those about cutting costs and improving operating margins

- an impact on staff morale and motivation where feelings of fear, uncertainty and doubt arise regarding their status and that of their teammates. (Depending on the circumstances and the nature of the change effort, this damage can linger as questions arise about the motivation of leadership and their commitment to staff wellbeing.)

- some of the wrong people stay and the right people go. Many good, experienced people in the company seek to leave as part of the downsizing or shortly after because they want to experience something new and fresh.

- the headline cuts and advertised savings end up being lost as companies hire consultants or outsource functions that can be more costly than they were in-house.

The world has changed and the pendulum has swung back to a different balance between growth and profit. Reducing expenditure in non-core activities and over-resourced business functions was a necessity. The reason to act was clear; however, the way savings are made in these circumstances deserves more thoughtful consideration than the broadly accepted view that it's a good thing to cut heads in this way.

Board Directors get off quite easily here, because restructuring charges and the impact on people are seen as the price of responding to investor/owner pressure.

I believe it's worth considering a more patient response to difficult situations, such as those encountered post the pandemic and during other downturns, to achieve reduced expenditure and resource levels. It is possible that with a more targeted approach to redundancies, natural attrition and better performance management actions, you can achieve expenses reductions and avoid some of the less obvious costs and damage of across-the-board redundancies. The BIG caveat here is that you need to have the balance sheet or the luxury (like most big tech) to fund a slightly slower path to reduced expenditure.

If you are not cash strapped, the merit of across-the-board cuts in headcount should be carefully compared against other alternatives that might take longer but cause less lasting impact.

It seems that many companies regretted the extent of their downsizing and cost-cutting during the 2008 recession, as they realised the negative long-term consequences for their talent, innovation and relationships with stakeholders.

In a survey conducted by McKinsey & Company (*McKinsey Quarterly*, 'A Better Way to Cut Costs', 2009), of the 79 per cent of companies that cut their costs, only 53 per cent of executives thought the measures helped their company weather the recession.

More recently, in an article from *Stanford News* from December 2022, Stanford Graduate School of Business Professor Jeffrey Pfeiffer described the tech industry layoffs as an instance of 'social contagion'. He said, 'Layoffs often do not cut costs, as there are many instances of laid off employees being hired back as contractors' and 'people don't pay attention to the evidence against layoffs'.

Where you can afford it, pushing back against 'social contagion' and shareholder pressure, and taking a more measured approach, is worth more consideration than it typically gets.

Making a next career move

After 14 years as a loyal 'IBMer', moving from General Manager of the IBM Personal Computer Division to Managing Director of Apple (ANZ) was a tough choice, as was moving from Vice President of Apple Australia to CEO of ninemsn — a role with smaller scope at a start-up backed by Apple's biggest competitor, Microsoft. But my hardest career choice was to leave my role at ninemsn to become Managing Director of Microsoft Australia.

I had been in the role for almost five years and felt the need to move on but was not clear about what I wanted to do and where I wanted to go. So much so that I paid an outplacement agency to run me through a process they provided people who were made redundant or in need of help to progress to the next stage of their career.

The approach aligns your head, heart and gut to guide you along potential pathways. It was an incredibly helpful process for me, and I have often used it to help others pondering a similar question about their next career move.

The process involves answering four key questions to identify your strengths and areas for development, and your likes and dislikes in a work environment to create decision criteria for your next career move.

> The Must-Do Toolbox in chapter 14 has the full list of questions, next steps and actions in the process.

Completing these steps helped me see two important things that pointed me in the direction of accepting the offer from Microsoft. First, I loved the culture of the US technology industry and wanted to work in it rather than that of Australian media companies in adjacent industries. Second, my daughters were old enough that I could travel and work overseas more, and Microsoft offered international opportunities that I had previously decided not to pursue. All this might seem obvious in hindsight, but at the time I was confused and unclear, and the process I followed helped me overcome that.

Final words on making hard choices

Making hard choices plays into the realm of all of the Must-Do actions, for example:

- **Must-Do #1 Apply the right mindset** — choosing to adopt the right mindset in the face of change when under personal pressure

- **Must-Do #2 Be self-aware** — choosing to hear and accept negative feedback without being defensive

- **Must-Do #5 Drive alignment** — choosing to move resources from one function to another to support the strategic direction

- **Must-Do #6 Focus on performance** — choosing to have a difficult conversation about someone's performance issues, rather than avoiding it.

A few things to keep in mind as you confront hard choices:

- Keep things in perspective. For most of us, hard choices at work are not a matter of life and death, unlike those working in the health and emergency services, for example. For most of us making hard choices at work doesn't close off the opportunity for course correction if we learn after the fact that adjustment is needed.

- There is a lot more to life than work, and the hard choices we make in our personal lives are often more difficult and important than those we make at work. In my experience, choices such as changing schools for an unhappy child or ending a long-term relationship involve more fear, uncertainty and doubt than hard choices faced at work.

- Face into the risks of the choice you are making and consider the worst thing that could happen if things go wrong. The short-term risk and pain are usually worth enduring to achieve a more sustainable, long-term outcome.

- A problem shared is a problem halved, so make sure to get advice from people less emotionally involved in the hard choice at hand.

Remember, deep down we sense when we should be making a hard choice but are avoiding it. Use that signal as motivation to push through. It will be worth it.

Chapter summary

Clarity, alignment and performance focus all depend on the quality of the hard choices we make. Hard choices are often 'between bad and badder'. Always try to show care for the people impacted.

Questions to ask yourself (or to ask others about you):

- What are the hard choices I may be avoiding or struggling with?

- Can someone with an objective or independent perspective help me?

- What could I do better to confront and make hard choices?

Recommended actions:

- Take time to make important decisions. Taking a bit longer is better than moving too soon. I've been told I can procrastinate, and that's true, but something inside me

(continued)

knows when I know enough and can move forward. We are all different in this regard.

- Seek advice from people around you, from those involved and from those who aren't involved and can be objective.

- Embrace contrarian views in shaping your own.

- Think about how the hard choice you make aligns with a bigger-picture, long-term objective, and with your values.

- Follow your gut feeling and your instincts. If it doesn't feel right, dig deeper into why.

- Don't seek perfection. The choice is hard because whichever way you go there will be negative consequences. Remember that you can adapt and correct course for mistakes and unexpected consequences. Often the reality isn't as bad as you feared.

- Take a breath and give yourself time alone to contemplate. It's amazing what pops into your head unexpectedly that can help with the decision.

Refer to the Must-Do Toolbox:

- Career counselling process.

PART IV

TAKE ACTION AND BE REWARDED

	Must-Do actions
BEING *Character*	1. Apply the <u>right mindset</u>
	2. Be <u>self-aware</u>
	3. <u>Care about people</u>
DOING *Words and actions*	4. Seek <u>clarity</u>
	5. Drive <u>alignment</u>
	6. Focus on <u>performance</u>
	7. <u>Have difficult conversations</u>
	8. <u>Make hard choices</u>

Part IV is your guide to putting the Must-Dos into action. Doing so will help you and those you work with better handle the shifts and shocks that lie ahead and have more fun at work!

The foundation for what follows is a commitment to continuous improvement driven by a healthy dissatisfaction with the way things are now. It is the commitment I described in the introduction that continuously works to address the gap between current reality and aspirations. I described this culture as one that doesn't spend much time celebrating success, instead quickly noting progress and moving on to the next challenge.

Your level of determination and commitment to closing the gap between current reality and your aspirations (and those of people around you) is the underlying driver of success in applying the eight Must-Dos.

The commitment you need to make to yourself and others is demonstrated by pursuing these five steps on the pathway to better performance:

1. Use the diagnostic tools provided to ask the right questions about current performance and what could be better.

2. Have a conversation with the people you work with about the diagnostic results, to identify the most important opportunities for improvement, and selecting a small number of problems you agree to fix. One thing at a time is a great start, so don't take on more than you can commit to work on.

3. Assign people to lead and support the work on the selected areas, making sure they can commit to complete it in the agreed timeframe.

4. Review progress at the end of the agreed timeframe.

5. Agree on further action that arises from the review of progress. If the action committed is completed, select the next opportunity for improvement to pursue and repeat steps 3 to 5. Doing so helps make getting better every day ingrained in team culture and how you work together.

After six months, redo the diagnostic to make sure the list derived from step 2 represents the most important areas to improve, given things can change.

Visit www.stevevamos.com to get further information and resources that complement the Playbooks and Tools in Chapters 13 and 14.

The Must-Do Diagnostic provides a holistic view of team performance and identifies the areas most in need of improvement. If you aren't ready to do the full diagnostic, you can make good progress by using the Performance to Potential Quick Diagnostic process from chapter 10.

You can also use that same quick diagnostic process with a question such as, 'How well aligned are we to execute our strategy?' or any of the questions that you are comfortable with from the Must-Do Diagnostic.

Chapter 13 includes playbooks that provide the recommended actions and tools to address areas that need improvement. Acting on any one Must-Do at a time will deliver benefits.

Two playbooks are provided for leaders of organisations, teams and change initiatives:

- the Being/Character Playbook

- the Doing/Words and Actions Playbook.

Actions and tools are also provided for:

- individual contributors/team members

- Board Directors.

Chapter 14 includes the Must-Do Toolbox, referenced throughout the book, with guides to help address a range of challenges your organisation or team may be facing.

The book concludes with chapter 15, *The journey is the reward*, and with *Final thoughts*, where I share the rewards of making the commitment to do the hard work of pursuing the eight Must-Dos.

CHAPTER 13

THE MUST-DO DIAGNOSTIC AND PLAYBOOKS

The Must-Do Diagnostic, Playbooks and Tools are the way to inspect the current state of your team and improve it. The best place to start is to have each member of the team complete the diagnostic shown in table 13.1 and be encouraged to respond honestly.

The Must-Do Diagnostic

I recommend using a trusted third party to facilitate the process, aggregate the scores and present them back to the team. Any team leader or individual member of a team can use the diagnostic to self-assess performance and identify the most significant opportunities for improvement.

The column on the right is for scoring each Must-Do to identify those most in need of attention and improvement. A score of over 75 total points is good to excellent, reflecting a well-led, high-performing team.

The diagnostic can highlight areas to further improve performance. Continuing to monitor performance using the diagnostic every six months will help identify any Must-Dos that are trending in the wrong direction. The results of this diagnostic can vary significantly from half year to half year as things change in team composition and operating environment. Don't take good results for granted.

A score between 60 and 74 is okay to good. Most good teams will rate themselves somewhere in this range; those scoring above 75 are rare in my experience. A team assessed in this range should have a conversation about the Must-Dos most in need of improvement. Improving one or two elements will make a difference.

A score of less than 60 indicates a need for discussion and action on several Must-Dos. Some difficult conversations and hard choices lie ahead for this team for performance to improve and change efforts to be successful. The drive and support of the team leader will be important when confronting the issues obstructing good performance. Assuming a leader and team members can have the difficult conversations required to address current obstacles, the pathway to a better place lies ahead.

Having a coach or objective third party involved in the improvement process can make a big difference, especially if the diagnostic highlights issues in the 'Being' domain, which can be sensitive given it reflects issues regarding the character and capability of the team leader. I touch on this area of sensitivity later in this chapter.

Use table 13.1 as a framework to consider and assess any team or change process you are part of at work or in life. Score each question based on how true the statement shown is for your team (0 = untrue, 10 = absolutely true).

Table 13.1: Must-Do Diagnostic

	Must-Do action	Diagnostic statement	Score*
BEING	**1. Apply the right mindset**	Our leader applies the right mindset to encourage and enable change because they accept mistakes as learning and value learning more than knowing.	/10
	2. Be self-aware	Our leader demonstrates self-awareness of their behaviour and their impact on others.	/10
		Our leader is a good listener who proactively seeks feedback, even if the news is not good.	/10
	3. Care about people	We feel safe to speak up and challenge the way we do things and to initiate change.	/10
		Our leader cares about people and developing talent.	/10
DOING	**4. Seek clarity**	Our purpose, priorities and expectations of how we behave and treat others are clear.	/10
	5. Drive alignment	We are well aligned to execute our strategy.	/10
	6. Focus on performance	We take action to review and improve performance.	/10
	7. Have difficult conversations	We have honest and direct conversations about the most difficult things.	/10
	8. Make hard choices	We make hard choices, that define where we do and don't focus our efforts and allocate resources.	/10
		Total score	**/100**

* 0 = untrue, 10 = absolutely true

The Being/Character Domain Playbook

This playbook (see table 13.2) provides the pathway to improving the Must-Dos of the Being/Character domain. As leader of your team, appreciate that the things that make change hard for people also make it hard for you. Your work and life experience shapes your character and influences your behaviour in the face of change.

The Being/Character Domain Playbook provides suggested actions and tools in each of the Must-Dos. I suggest you pick the action/tool that resonates most with the Must-Do the diagnostic and other feedback has indicated needs the most attention.

Seek help from others to hold you accountable for each action, and where appropriate get help from a coach. Remember, being 'coachable' is a great asset. It means:

- being willing to accept the views of others as their reality, even if you don't like or agree with them

- being willing to change your opinion or course based on the suggestions of others

- proactively seeking and accepting feedback and ways to learn and improve

- listening actively, without being defensive.

Table 13.2: Must-Do Playbook — Being/Character domain

Must-Do	Actions to take — tools to use
1. Apply the right mindset	• Use figure 5.1 as a tool to remind you of the difference between a fixed/default mindset and one that is open to change. Print it, put it on your wall and consider what mindset you are demonstrating at different times through the day, particularly when you are under stress. • Recognise and face into your fears and those of others around you. Talk about what is behind those fears and how they can be allayed if possible. Just discussing them can help a lot.

Must-Do	Actions to take — tools to use

2. Be self-aware	Understand how life experience has shaped you; study, read, and seek coaching, counsel and feedback to do the work on yourself. Explore the source of any insecurities you have that will trigger the wrong mindset and behaviour when confronted with tense situations and change.
	
	- Refer to books like *Do the Work* by Nicole LePera and do the exercises if you feel they could help.
	
	Develop your own rules, prompts and tools to help you pause in the moment between an emotion and a reaction.
	
	    For example, be mindful by observing yourself as you would an actor in a movie or play; take a breath before you react and speak; commit yourself to rules such as never thinking something is stupid until you fully understand it.
	
	Proactively seek feedback that can help you develop/improve. For example, ask people:
	
	- 'What did I miss or what could I do better?' and then add, 'What else?'
	- 'Do you think I am a control freak?'
	- 'Am I a good listener or do I talk too much?'
	
	    You can also use the *Do More/Do Less* feedback exercise (Chapter 6).
	
	Get a coach for your team who can observe how you work together and facilitate conversations about how that can improve (and *you* can improve).

3. Care about people	Show you care about people and talent by: - encouraging good people leadership by providing the right feedback loops and clear performance expectations - not allowing persistently poor-performing people leaders and individual contributors to remain in those roles - behaving like a head coach, investing time to build great teams - coaching self-centred people and encouraging them to understand what drives their behaviour (see Must-Do 2) - proactively seeking feedback on how the organisation or your team can develop/improve (especially things you might not want to hear), as a way of making it safe for people to speak the truth. Use the nine-box talent management tool (Toolbox).

The road to higher performance can be uncomfortable and personally challenging if your team feel you are weak in this domain.

If you are the leader inviting your team to do the diagnostic, that's a good sign. If the scores indicate improvement is required, make sure you encourage team members to speak honestly about how you can be a better leader.

Receiving negative feedback is never easy, but the benefit of listening and accepting another's truth, being vulnerable and asking for help is a gift and will serve to help you be at your best. This process clears the air and can win hearts and minds as you demonstrate your willingness to listen and improve. Everyone benefits.

The Doing/Words and Actions Domain Playbook

This playbook (see table 13.3) provides the pathway to improving in the Must-Do areas of Doing/Words and Actions.

Table 13.3: Must-Do Playbook — Doing/Words and Actions Domain

Must-Do	Actions to take — tools to use
4. Seek clarity	As the leader of an organisation or team, you can't allow lack of clarity to get in the way of your people. While absolute clarity is never possible, you can be vigilant in dealing with the issues of clarity that you and your team members experience.
	• Ask the hard questions regarding clarity of purpose (see Chapter 8).
	• Ask 'what is possible?' to start your planning process and when setting goals.
	• Run the Performance to Potential Quick Diagnostic (see Chapter 10).
	• Fast-track clarity of priorities (Toolbox).
	• Create a team code and live it (Toolbox).
	• Involve people in the process of establishing Values and Behaviours to counter known dysfunction.

Must-Do	Actions to take — tools to use
5. Drive alignment	As team leaders, we need to invest the time to make sure all our team members' objectives are aligned with our most important priorities. For organisation leaders, this means driving alignment across and through the organisation on the initiatives that matter most. • Run the 'How well are we aligned?' version of the Performance to Potential Quick Diagnostic and commit to fixing the most significant issues raised. • Implement level order planning where top-level priorities are cascaded across and through your organisation (Toolbox). • Building great products requires great cross-functional collaboration; strengthen alignment in product management (Toolbox). • Bring technology prioritisation decisions to the top team meetings.
6. Focus on performance	Being focused on performance is the way to help increase clarity and adjust alignment given experience and changing operating conditions • Use the performance review process to adjust where you are heading (clarity) and how you are executing (alignment). • Establish a good rhythm of the business (chapter 10). • Do the Must-Do Diagnostic or the Performance to Potential Quick Diagnostic (Chapter 10) on a six-monthly cycle. • Provide people leader performance feedback and prioritise the importance of being an effective people leader. • Make sure all team members receive honest performance feedback. • Ensure people managers confront performance issues of their team members and deal with them professionally (Toolbox).

(continued)

Must-Do	Actions to take — tools to use
7. Have difficult conversations	Set an example by encouraging (not avoiding) difficult conversations: • Practise with feedback speed dating (Toolbox). • Study the how to have a difficult conversation (Chapter 11 on clear context, care, courage). • Confront individual performance issues with the guide provided (Toolbox). • Run training for your organisation or team, and refer to resources such as *Radical Candor* by Kim Scott.
8. Make hard choices	Consider the hard choices you may be avoiding or struggling with, and whether someone objective or independent can help. • Ask those who work with you if you can do better to confront and make hard choices. • Take time to make important decisions. A bit longer can be better than too soon, as long as it isn't too long. • Embrace contrarian views in shaping your view. • Think about how the hard choice you make aligns with a bigger-picture, long-term objective and your values. • Follow your gut feeling and instincts; if it doesn't feel right, dig deeper into why. • Don't seek perfection. The choice is hard because whichever way you go may have a downside or negative consequences. Remember you can adapt and correct course for mistakes and unexpected fallout, and that the reality is often not as bad as you fear. • Make sure to take a breath and give yourself time alone to contemplate. It's amazing what pops into your head that can help when you don't expect it. • When relevant, reference the 'Career counselling' guide (Toolbox).

Notes for an individual contributor

As an individual team member, you can use the two previous playbooks to encourage actions from your team leader and other members of your team to help improve performance.

The road to improved performance can be challenging if your team leader is weak in the Being/Character domain. Often this weakness can make it hard to get clear and aligned, or to have difficult conversations and make hard choices. For example, an overly self-centred or insecure leader is less likely to create a safe environment for challenge and change for you and your team members.

If you are a member of a team and are considering the diagnosis without the knowledge or involvement of your leader, and you see weakness in Being or character, the journey is complex. The question arises, is it reasonable to expect your leader to be part of the solution? The path forward depends on how coachable your team leader is and how safe it is for you and other team members to provide feedback or encourage the leader to seek it.

If for any reason raising the issues directly with your team leader isn't an option, change will be hard without intervention. This intervention may need to come from the manager of the leader or in the case of a CEO, a Board Director or owner of the organisation. Unfortunately, this may occur only when performance issues surrounding the team or change effort become acute and visible.

I try to encourage people who have bosses with issues in the Being Must-Dos to have the courage to constructively raise the issue with their boss, or to find ways to get the message to their boss's boss, if they have one. If their boss dislikes the message or retaliates in some way, the person providing the feedback is probably best moving somewhere else to work. I appreciate this is much easier to say than do.

If the Being/Character domain is too sensitive, another approach is to diagnose and discuss improvements in the Doing/Words and Actions domain while others resolve the leadership issue. The reality is that any improvement in these Must-Dos will benefit the team and change program concerned, even though weakness in the Being/Character domain might continue to be a limiting factor of performance.

Coaching can also make a big difference here. Finding a way to have your team leader seek that support is a good idea but often hard to suggest.

Individual contributor actions and tools

The following actions and tools can help you on your journey to lead positive change around you.

Know and develop yourself

- Understand how life experience has shaped you. Study, read, and seek coaching/counsel/feedback to do the work on yourself. Explore the source of any insecurities you have that could trigger the wrong mindset and behaviour when confronted with tense situations and change. Read books like *Do the Work* by Nicole LePera and do the exercises.

- Develop your own rules, prompts and tools to help you pause in the moment between an emotion and a reaction. For example, be mindful by observing yourself as you would an actor in a movie or play. Take a breath before you react and speak. Commit yourself to rules such as never thinking something is stupid until you fully understand it.

- Use figure 5.1 as a tool. Print it out, put it on your wall and reflect throughout the day on what mindset you are demonstrating.

Find your purpose and ambition

- Make sure your purpose (why you do what you do) stays relevant.

- Aspire to be better and do better every day.

- Consider how much of your time each day is spent in the *why* and *how* you do what you do, rather than doing *what* you do.

- MUST DO 8#: 'Making a next career move' (Chapter 12)

Develop your skills to have difficult conversations and make hard choices

- Do training on 'How to have difficult conversations' (refer to resources such as Kim Scott and courses on having crucial conversations).

- MUST DO 8#: Make hard choices (Chapter 12)

- MUST DO 7#: Have difficult converations (Chapter 11)

- TOOL: Practise feedback speed dating (Toolbox).

Notes for a Board Director

The Must-Do Diagnostic and Playbooks provide a way for Board Directors to understand the character and capability of their CEO and leadership team and to help them improve.

The road to strong organisation and team performance can be challenging if the CEO is weak in any of the Must-Dos of the Being/Character domain. This weakness will impact the leadership team's ability to get clear and aligned or to have difficult conversations and make hard choices. An overly self-centred or insecure CEO is less likely to create a safe environment for challenge and change. It is important the Board understands these issues and encourages the CEO to develop themselves in this domain.

Coaching and feedback can make a difference. Encourage the organisation leader to seek support by finding a good coach for themselves and the leadership team. A strong HR lead can make a big difference too.

The following actions and tools from this book can help a Board Director in their role.

Understand leadership team performance by demanding the right diagnostics.

- See the Xero TeamX example that follows.

- The Performance to Potential Quick Diagnostic (Chapter 10)

- Must-Do Diagnostic (chapter 13)

Build your capability to have difficult conversations and make hard choices

- Do training on how to have difficult conversations' (refer to Kim Scott and *Radical Candor*).

- MUST DO 8#: Make hard choices (Chapter 12)

- MUST DO 7#: Have difficult converations (Chapter 11)

- Practise feedback speed dating (Toolbox).

Look for the following in developing and executing strategy

- Make sure your organisation's purpose — why you do what you do — is not losing relevance.

- Look for ambition and aspiration to be better and do better in plans.

- Make sure priorities are clear and there is a focus on the few most important ones.

- Ask the questions about clarity of purpose on (Chapter 8).

- Demand the CEO implement level order planning or a similar process (Toolbox).

Know and develop yourself:

- Understand how life experience has shaped you; study, read, and seek coaching/counsel/feedback to do the work on yourself to explore the source of any insecurities you have that will trigger the wrong mindset and behaviour when confronted with tense situations and change. Read books like *Do the Work* by Nicole LePera and do the exercises.

- Develop your own rules, prompts and tools to help you pause in the moment between an emotion and a reaction. For example, be mindful by observing yourself as you would an actor in a movie or play. Take a breath before you react and speak, and commit to never thinking something is stupid until you fully understand it.

- Use figure 5.1 as a tool, print it, put it on your wall and reflect through the day on what mindset you are demonstrating.

Case study: Xero's TeamX Diagnostic

At Xero, we created the TeamX Diagnostic, based on several of the Must-Dos. A sample of what the Board received is shown in figure 13.1 (note that the results are examples only). The scores showed team members' collective level of agreement with the diagnostic statements for each factor. The trends and the conversation we had as a team regarding our performance was what delivered value. This data also formed the basis of a conversation with the Board about the areas where I had to improve team performance and my own performance.

Key factors	Dec '21	May '22	Dec '22
Psychological safety	52%	66%	73%
Difficult conversations and hard choices	25%	44%	40%
Clarity	73%	81%	79%
Alignment	59%	77%	59%
Focus on performance	56%	67%	77%

Figure 13.1: Xero TeamX Diagnostic

What does success look like?

In the face of change and inevitable future shifts and shocks, the Must-Do Diagnostic, Playbooks and Tools provide a pathway to improve the quality of organisation and team performance. A fair question to ask is, *what does success look like?*

First three to six months

Positive outcomes to look for in the short term start with improvement in team morale and wellbeing. These gains come from increased team cohesion as a result of being honest about what's wrong, addressing the issues and working better together. Progress is seen in employee engagement or net promoter scores.

Improvement will also be evident in the leading indicators of operational performance that reflect the quality of work being done to produce longer-term results. This improvement comes because the obstacles to people doing their best work are reduced if the team is committed to addressing known issues.

Six months and beyond

In the longer term the improvement in team performance becomes evident in stronger financial results reflecting better execution of strategy and improvement in operations. Other benefits include:

- greater relevance to customers, producing a higher customer Net Promoter Score, revenue growth and higher retention rates

- greater relevance and attractiveness to talent, as your employment brand strengthens.

Final words on the Must-Do Diagnostic and playbooks

Achieving the benefits of improving in the Must-Dos takes time and commitment to having difficult conversations that identify and confront areas of poor performance and taking action to fix them.

Small steps can make a big difference and doing any one of the following three things each day can become a habit that leads to very positive outcomes.

1. Think about how you think, by observing yourself in action.

2. Do one thing to improve how you and others are working together.

3. Have a difficult conversation you might be avoiding.

Apple and Microsoft have demonstrated at scale over the past two decades that despite how difficult and challenging things can get, with strong leadership, teamwork and effective change, great outcomes are possible. In chapter 15 I talk about the rewards that flow from the commitment and doing the hard work to be better every day.

Chapter summary

Start by diagnosing how you and your team are tracking against each of the Must-Dos. With clear assessment you can move forward with the right conversations to formulate actions needed to improve in the Must-Dos most needing attention.

Recommended actions:

- Assess your team or change program using the Must-Do Diagnostic, and refer to the recommendations and tools suggested to address the weakest areas.

- Pay attention to the score on Being/Character, as a low score on this element indicates the leader needs help and coaching.

- Engage an external coach and benefit from objective third-party expertise and facilitation.

- If you are a Board Director or individual contributor, use the actions and tools suggested as a guide to how you can contribute to improving your organisation or team performance and to developing yourself.

- Think of the eight Must-Dos as levers you can pull to improve performance. Improvement in any single area has benefits you will see and feel.

CHAPTER 14

THE MUST-DO TOOLBOX

This chapter presents the how-to guides referenced throughout the book. These tools (table 14.1) have served me well in dealing with the shifts and shocks over the years.

I don't take credit for developing any of these tools; they reflect my learning from great Human Resources people, consultants and books I have read. In their current form they reflect how I have adapted them over the years.

Rather than read through all the tools in this chapter, focus on the ones that help most in areas that will benefit you, your team or change initiative.

Table 14.1: tools and associated benefits

Tool #	Tool name	Benefits
1	Confront individual performance issues	A guide to having the difficult conversation with someone about their performance, in a caring way
2	Practise feedback speed dating	A way for team members to improve their relationships and self-awareness, by giving honest feedback on performance and showing care and appreciation of each other
3	Fast-track clarity of priorities in 1–2 days	A fast way to bring a team together to get clear and aligned to achieve their collective objectives

(continued)

Tool #	Tool name	Benefits
4	Develop a team code and live by it	A process to make behavioural standards clear and team members more self-aware by setting standards and providing feedback
5	Implement level order planning	The planning process that is critical to driving clarity, alignment and encouraging difficult conversations and hard choices
6	Align to be a better product business	A guide to managing and measuring the quality of cross functional alignment that is key to delivering a great product or service
7	Implement a nine-box talent management tool	A process to assess and develop people across an organisation or team and encourage the conversation about the quality of talent
8	Career counselling process	A process to help people consider and make hard choices about their career path

1. Confront individual performance issues

Among the toughest things people leaders must do is confront and deal with performance issues of their team members. Having the right mindset before you start the process is important. Make sure to come to the meeting with a clear head, well prepared, and with the intent to help both the person concerned and your organisation.

> *There are good reasons why we have two ears and only one mouth. Be ready to really listen.*

The following steps have worked well for me.

Step 1: Listen and understand why the person is not performing well

Try your best to understand the 'heart and head' of the person concerned. The more they speak, the better. Listen and suspend judgement.

A good opening question in such discussions is to ask simply, 'How are you feeling about the job?' or 'Are you enjoying the job?'

There are many possible reasons for poor performance and each demands a clear understanding to establish the right course of action. Common causes include the following:

- personal issues such as poor health, or family or relationship problems

- lack of skills or experience to do the job

- lack of adequate direction and clarity about what is expected. It is important not to underestimate the impact that this can cause. (As manager you need to be open to and recognise your contribution to problems experienced by team members, if expectations have not been set clearly.)

- poor culture fit, meaning the person's behaviour is not consistent with what is aspired to and expected by the organisation.

  Team members who lack people relationship skills can fall into this category. They might possess more than adequate technical skills, but their interpersonal skills are the area of concern. Make sure expected behaviours are well explained so efforts to improve are clear.

  You need to use real examples of what the person is doing wrong to help them understand the need for change. Try not to be judgemental; couch your feedback in a way that allows for better understanding of what is behind the problem.

Case study: Confronting performance issues

Some time ago one of the most talented members of my team had an aspect of her performance that was limiting her potential. She needed to constantly demonstrate that she was right when challenged by others. She also had a short fuse under pressure or when being questioned, and needed to frequently prove her worth and knowledge.

(continued)

While everyone could see her talent and capability, they also experienced the negative effects of these attributes and the impact on their working relationship with her.

We sat down together and had a long conversation in which we touched on the unproductive behaviours and discussed the source. This related to a childhood and adolescence lacking in parental acknowledgement or recognition — unfortunately not uncommon. She was triggered by anything that arose in the workplace that threatened her sense of self-worth.

I talked to her about how the behaviour was going to limit her career unless she resolved the source of it or addressed the symptoms. We agreed to reconvene and discuss it again after she had time to contemplate further.

When we next met, she told me that she could not address the source of the issue because of the depth of the associated trauma, but she made a commitment that she would manage the behaviour going forward. She did this by introducing a mindfulness practice (a breathing exercise) when she felt the old response was being triggered.

I was blown away by the quality of the change. I was also proud to watch her go on and have a great executive career.

- Perhaps they are burnt out or have just been around too long. Employees who have experienced many ups and downs in the life of the business, or who have been around a long time, can lose their motivation and enthusiasm. This state of 'spiritual bankruptcy' is very hard to turn around.

  The symptoms typically displayed are a negative attitude, which concentrates on what's wrong rather than what's right about the business. Once an employee reaches this state it is very difficult to turn the situation around. Despite their positive contribution in the past, the right thing is usually for the person to move on. They just need help to see it, confront it and accept that their future will be better elsewhere.

Case study: Knowing when your time is up

On another occasion, one of the longest serving senior leaders of the organisation I led, a very talented, experienced and funny person, was frustrated and dissatisfied with her role and opportunities for advancement at the company. It was early in my time in the leadership role, and we had already had some conversations about their need to think about the next career steps outside the company.

At a company meeting, with several hundred people present, I was outlining ways we would move forward, when I encouraged questions and comments from the audience. At this invitation, she stood up and told me that some of what I was saying was just bullshit. I welcomed the honesty and wasn't too bothered by the directness, but others who observed it later commented negatively to me about what happened.

Without requesting a meeting, she came into my office to apologise and added, 'It's really time for me to go.' The resignation followed shortly after. Unsurprisingly, she moved on to have a great career in the international telco and media industry as a senior executive and CEO.

Sometimes when their time is up, people don't see it. In this person's case they did see it and (despite the meeting outburst) responded professionally.

- Sometimes changes in their role may leave a team member behind. With business changing so fast, good people who once served us well in the past can become less suited to the jobs into which their roles evolve. This happens in fast and high-growth companies, where over a five-year period the needs and nature of a senior role can change substantially. It's a tough problem to solve and the solutions are not always obvious or easy. If the person has a good attitude, it makes sense to work hard to find a new role for them.

Step 2: Establish clear expectations

After identifying the factors affecting performance, the next step is to document the areas of concern and actions to be taken to improve performance. Provide plenty of examples of actions or behaviours expected so the team member understands clearly what's expected. Be direct and honest about the consequences of not addressing performance issues adequately.

From the outset, use words that describe the consequences, such as, 'If we don't see significant progress over the next two months then we will need to formally review your suitability for this role.' This will clarify the seriousness of the situation.

There are softer ways to start out on this path, which reflect that you are hoping the employee will be able to step up, or that the changes to the role, or some other aspects of the work, are successful. Show you care about the person by saying, 'It isn't good for you or the business to sustain a situation where both parties are not in a good place.'

Step 3: Provide frequent feedback

The more frequent the feedback provided to the person, the better. Selecting the right time and place to give someone feedback is important. Ensure that feedback sessions are held in a private office or meeting room and that adequate time is made for discussions without interruption.

Seek feedback from other team members to help make the issues clearer to the employee or to help improve performance.

Step 4: Draw the process to a conclusion

Set an agreed and reasonable concluding date, which will vary depending on circumstances. Hopefully, performance has improved or the team member comes to recognise that they are not a good fit for the role and agree to move into a new position or leave the business.

If the process is progressing towards a termination, involve the HR manager or another senior manager in the process. Involving another manager ensures that if for any reason the individual concerned decides to challenge the process formally, the business has two people who can confirm the fair treatment of the team member.

Throughout the process always be sure to acknowledge the good things about the person that you appreciate about them and their contribution to the business.

Step 5: Treat departing people respectfully

If the process ends in a parting of ways, allow the person to leave the business with dignity. Treating people in a fair and respectful manner at this point is an important signal that the company does care about its people.

Given that the departing team member may well remain in the industry or end up being employed by a customer or supplier, maintaining good relationships as much as possible is good business practice and common sense as well as being ethically the right thing to do.

On termination, always pay the employee their entitlements and, if possible, a little more than is legally required as an act of good faith.

Let the person finish up with a reasonable notice period that allows them to say farewell and hand over any work in progress. I really dislike the practice of escorting dismissed staff off the premises. If you could trust them before they resigned, surely you can trust them to leave in the right way. This makes people who stay feel a lot better about you and the company they work for.

Allow them to provide input on the way their reasons for departure are communicated.

Don't make promises about providing a reference without making it clear what will and won't be said to prospective employers. If you can't tell the truth, then best not to comment. This approach will help the person position their previous work experience in the most appropriate way with prospective new employers.

From my experience, assuming you are genuine and caring in the process, more than 80 per cent of the people you move on will end up thanking you for it, because it opens doors to better-suited positions elsewhere; 20 per cent will be angry or dislike you forever. Unfortunately, managing people is not a popularity contest. It's also important to note that the business also benefits immediately when these issues are confronted promptly with professionalism and sensitivity.

2. Practise feedback speed dating

Feedback speed dating is a great exercise for teams to practise having conversations that help individual team members improve how they engage with each other.

Step 1

Put feedback speed dating on the agenda of your monthly or quarterly team meeting.

Step 2

Pair people up to have the feedback conversation in the style of speed dating.

Step 3

Over a 10-minute conversation, each person has five minutes to answer the following about the other:

- The things I really appreciate that you bring to the team and the business are ...

- The things I think we could do better to improve how we work together are ...

Step 4

Move on to new pairs and repeat Step 3.

• • •

The benefits of this exercise are twofold:

- Team members sharing appreciation of each other's skills and contribution is a positive way to build relationships.

- Feedback speed dating provides practice for giving feedback on areas for improvement in a relatively safe environment, with clear positive intent.

3. Fast-track clarity of priorities in 1–2 days

A great way to drive clarity is to conduct a well-structured one- to two-day meeting with the leadership group or team that focuses on pressing issues and priorities for action. It's a good way to fast-track 80 per cent of the most important things you derive from a longer, more detailed strategy process.

This exercise is one I have run many times, and it works. You should still do a solid top-down strategy with the other 20 per cent in mind, because this process is more focused on extracting what people think and know today, rather than considering the wide range of influences and change that can impact an organisation in the future.

Step 1

Arrange an offsite meeting with the top one or two management layers of people in your organisation. For a smaller organisation or team this can be the CEO or team leader and their direct reports. Also, as appropriate, invite some additional key people.

Step 2

Prepare an agenda that looks like the example below. For a large organisation two days may be required, so increase the meeting time of each session depending on your needs. The agenda items below cover most of the elements demanding clarity. Only include those items where clarity does not exist. Table 14.2 (overleaf) shows an example offsite meeting agenda.

Table 14.2: example offsite meeting agenda

8:00	Session 1: Welcome, agenda, objectives
8:30	Session 2: Ground rules and check-in
9:30	Session 3: Purpose, priorities and goals — discussion and Q&A
11:00	Session 4: Performance to Potential Quick Diagnostic and discussion
1:00	Session 5: Priority-setting workshop
3:30	Session 6: Team code workshop
5:00	Session 7: Rhythm of the business discussion
6:00	Session 8: Close

Step 3

Run the meeting with an objective facilitator so all team members can participate fully, and all participants are heard. Following are more details regarding each item on the agenda, and how to conduct the sessions on the day:

- **Session 1.** Welcome, agenda, objectives [usually covered by the CEO or team leader]

- **Session 2.** Ground rules and check-in [each attendee answers these questions]

    o   How are you feeling coming into this meeting?

    o   Is there anything you want to make sure is discussed today?

    o   Is there anything stopping you from being fully present in the meeting?

- **Session 3.** Purpose, priorities and goals — discussion and Q&A

    The CEO or team leader should prepare or present the most recent information on the following topics (consider it a 'state of the nation' review).

    o   Business environment and performance update/external context/outline

- o Current and new purpose [if change is proposed]

- o Goals and aspirations [for the relevant timeframe]

- o Priorities going forward [team leader view]

- o Q&A and discussion time

- **Session 4.** Performance to Potential Quick Diagnostic and discussion of the score

  - o Assess the team's current view of performance to potential, with the resources available as per the diagnostic in Chapter 10.

  - o Discuss the results and agree to action *one thing that could make a biggest difference.*

- **Session 5.** Priority-setting (workshop)

  - o Discuss this question: 'What are the top five things we need to do to execute our strategy and achieve our ambitions?'

  - o Have each person write down their top five items on Post-it notes.

  - o Have everyone present their top five to the group. As they are called out, have the facilitator group similar items on a whiteboard.

  - o Have participants vote on the top three to five.

  - o Assign the right people to lead these efforts and further define the required contribution of team members to action.

  - o Build regular follow-up of progress into the agenda of all future team meetings.

- **Session 6.** Team code workshop

  Refer to details of Tool #4.

- **Session 7.** Rhythm of the business

  o   Are our meetings productive and of good quality?

  o   Are they held at the right time and with the right agenda?

  o   If not, when should we meet and what agendas should we set for our meetings?

- **Session 8.** Close (team leader summary of actions and next steps)

4. Develop a team code and live by it

The 'values and behaviours' of an organisation provide clarity for how people should behave and treat those they work with, regardless of their role and the team they work on.

Another practice I encourage is developing a team code. A team code is a behavioural code specific to a team that defines how they work together. Individuals and teams across an organisation differ in the work they do and how they work. Establishing clarity of expectations for all members of a team helps improve performance.

The Xero leadership team developed a team code that we committed to live by. The steps to develop the team code were straightforward.

Step 1

List the good things about working as a team that each member of the team feels are great and should never be lost.

Step 2

List the things about working as a team that can drive members of the team crazy and need to change.

Step 3

Vote on the most important things to address and then consolidate them into a code of four to six key things that maintain the best and address the worst qualities.

The output of the Xero exercise was:

- *The C-team is my primary team.*

- *I support and care about my team members.*

- *I talk face to face about issues and avoid backchanneling.*

- *I listen to others and give/receive feedback respectfully.*

- *I build a strong team that frees me up to be an effective C-team leader.*

- *I regularly communicate the importance of the Xero priorities and actions, putting them ahead of functional, individual objectives.*

The six points in Xero's C-Team Code are aspirational statements that became expectations. By living this code, the team had clarity about expectations of how they worked together. Once a team code is developed there are two things that can be done to ensure the team lives by it:

1. Check in quarterly as a team to discuss which areas of the team code are being lived and which ones need improvement. For those that need improvement, discuss if there is something that can be done to improve it. Pick one action that arises and make it happen. Review if that one thing was done at the next monthly meeting or check-in.

2. Give each other individual feedback. Anonymously rate each member of the team against each team code attribute. Rate them as:

   ◊ **(R)ole model** means they are standouts in how they live the attribute

- o **(A)cceptable** means they demonstrate the attribute adequately

- o **(D)eveloping** means they are still building capability in the attribute.

The feedback an individual receives may look like table 14.3. Note that all team members self-assess and rate all other members of the team.

Table 14.3: feedback rating chart

	Team member self-assessment	Aggregated feedback from other team members
Team code attribute 1	A	A
Team code attribute 2	A	D
Team code attribute 3	D	A
Team code attribute 4	R	R
Team code attribute 5	A	A

Take note of where self-assessment as a team member is consistent with the view of other team members providing feedback and where it differs. Keeping this feedback confidential is important, so have an independent person collate and distribute the feedback.

In this example, in attribute 2 the team member has rated themselves much higher than their peers rated them, and in attribute 3 the team member rated themselves lower than others did.

Performing this exercise in a safe environment can lead to healthy conversations about expectations and individual performance that can contribute to a better team experience.

5. Implement level order planning

As discussed in chapter 9, level order planning is a process by which strategy is translated into real objectives and actions that are:

- clearly worded

- measurable with identified leaders and supporters

- cascaded level by level into the organisation as the top-level objectives and actions get broken down into specific lower-level actions

- synchronised across the organisation to ensure that actions relying on cross-functional cooperation and collaboration produce the desired outcome.

Level order planning helps define the HOW of strategy.

The process of level order planning can vary from organisation to organisation, depending on the size and scale. An organisation of fewer than 100 people won't need as much documentation or time invested in the process.

The fundamental principle of the process is to make sure that strategy is far more than *why* we need to do the things we want and *what* we need to do. Strategy is also clear about *how* we are going to do it. Nailing the how forces the following questions to be discussed:

- Who is going to lead or do this?

- Whose help do they need?

- Are the resources and skills in place?

- Are we organised the best way to execute the strategy?

- How do we know if we are making progress?

Without a process that drives strategic intent into a set of clear coordinated, cross-business actions that define how we execute our strategy, the misalignment between what we do today and where we want to be in the future is hard to overcome.

The level order planning process is not easy. It requires persistence and commitment. Typically, leaders don't like getting bogged down in detail. This is why strategy execution can often fail. The devil is in the detail.

In my experience, the single most important aspect of making level order planning work is the commitment of the CEO or organisation's leader to the process. Also important is assigning a capable person to steer the process and hold everyone accountable to deliver on each of the following steps in the timeframes set. The person can be of any professional background if they have the respect of those they work with and good project management skills.

Level order planning defines the strategy execution scorecard and review meeting agenda.

An important output of level order planning is the scorecard created that lists the strategies, objectives, and KPIs or metrics/measures of progress.

You can use a simple red/yellow/green traffic light, or actual metrics to track progress. A qualitative statement of progress can also be used for those objectives that are not as easily quantified (for example, completed/on-track/behind).

The Top Level 1 Strategies/Objectives should feature strongly in the agenda of leadership and management team meetings because they are the things that matter most to executing strategy.

Prioritise discussion of those areas that are not performing to expectation so remediation plans can be put in place.

Assuming you have developed a strategy that has up to five or six priorities, here is an example of how one of those is further defined and cascaded using Level Order Planning.

Step 1

First make sure you are clear about the high-level details of the strategic priority, in this case: To 'improve customer experience'.

- Name and number: Strategic Priority 1 'Improve customer experience'

- Measure: Increase NPS by five points

- Leader: Chief Customer Officer

- Supporters: Head of Operations, IT and Manufacturing

Step 2

The leader and supporters executing this strategy involve their direct reports in defining the objectives (call them actions if you wish). For example, the objectives/actions to execute strategic priority 1 are:

- 1A Implement a new CRM system.

- 1B Improve skills and capabilities to serve customers.

- 1C Improve product development process to better consider customer feedback.

Step 3

Each of these objectives must be clear, defined by measurable actions, and have a leader and supporters assigned to execute. For example, Objective 1A:

- Name and number: Objective 1A 'Implement a new CRM system'

- Measure: New CRM deployed successfully by December 2024 within agreed budget

- Leader: Chief Customer Officer

- Supporters: Head of Operations, Head of Information Technology

Step 4

Define the actions to execute the objective.

Continuing to use the example Objective 1A, the actions to execute are:

- 1A1 Develop clear and agreed specifications/requirements.
- 1A2 Prepare and issue tender document for software and implementation services.
- 1A3 Select preferred solution.
- 1A4 Define implementation plan.
- 1A5 Execute implementation plan.

Step 5

For each of these actions assign:

- a clear measure of success
- a leader and supporters to get the job done
- details of the resources (money and people) and timeframe needed to get it done.

Step 6

As the process evolves, each strategy and its associated objectives, actions and resources required must be reviewed with the leadership group and classified as:

- A. defined and committed to be executed
- B. not yet defined and committed (work in progress due to be completed by a specified date)
- C. defined but not committed due to resource constraints or other issues.

Discussion regarding those defined as 'C' is vital because this is where prioritisation happens. If the process has integrity, then these items are resolved as follows:

- A. Resources are allocated or added to get the action executed.

- B. The action is deferred or ruled out due to lack of priority and available resources.

● ● ●

The level order planning process requires discipline and diligence. I recommend its use for the most important strategies and objectives that the organisation must execute.

6. Align to be a better product business

The 'virtuous cycle' of product management (see figure 14.1) is fundamental to success whether you are a large corporation or a start-up. There is no fixed organisational model for great product management, because the most effective approach must be suited to the people and business circumstances of each organisation or business venture.

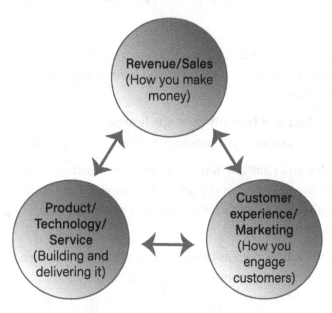

Figure 14.1: virtuous cycle of product management

Different product management processes can exist in one organisation for different needs; for example, a process for a start-up or new product business can operate on a different cycle from one for an established or mature product business.

The person playing the central, coordinating role—often called the Product Manager—ensures that the organisation senses customer feedback, market and technology changes, and responds quickly with the right product or service model changes that will deliver the desired customer experience and revenue outcome. As more business is done digitally, customer feedback is more easily sourced by tracking customer usage of the product or service.

The Product Manager needs to be a strong cross-functional collaborator and a fast learner, receptive to the views of others and to changes happening around them.

Making sure you continually get the right product to the right customer, at the right price and place, is one of the most challenging functions of business and demands the bridging of several functions.

The three broad functions at the heart of good product business management are:

1. **marketing**—the function that leads the definition of which customer or market segment you are looking to address with a solution to a need or problem

2. **product and technology**—the functions in your business that design and build the products and services you provide

3. **sales and channel management**—the functions responsible for the monetisation of the product or service and the distribution channels needed to get the product or service to the target customer or market.

I refer to these functions as the three legs of a stool. Failure or weakness in any one area can impact success dramatically.

One way to assess the current quality of the interplay of these functions in your organisation, to make it measurable and form a basis for improvement, involves the following steps.

Step 1

Rate the individual capability of the leaders of each of the three functional areas on any scale you prefer. If there is more than one person in each function, measure them both and average the score. Calculate the overall functional average score. (For example, on a scale of 1 to 10 it might look like: Sales 7/10, Marketing 8/10, Product 6/10 = *Functional Average of 7/10*.)

Step 2

Rate the quality of the *relationships* between the leaders of each of the functions. Calculate the average score. (For example, Sales–Marketing Relationship scores 5/10, Marketing–Product 6/10, Sales–Product 7/10 = *Relationship Average of 6/10*.)

Step 3

Calculate your overall product business management quality score, which is:

(1 × (functional average score) + 2 × (relationship score))/3

Or, in the example above,

((7) + (2 × 6))/3 = 6.33

The score provides a pathway to identify where the weakest links are in the capabilities and relationships of the functions involved in making sure the organisation can respond to change in market conditions and customer expectations with new products and services.

The person most responsible for the commercial success of the product or service is accountable for the overall score. In an early-stage business that is likely to be the CEO. In order to improve the score, that leader should consider and act on the following questions:

Could the process of product business management be better if:

1. I helped improve the skills/performance/relationships of any of the leaders or changed personnel?

2. I spent more time helping them get aligned with each other and the big-picture priorities of the organisation?

Ultimately, great product is all about having the right people in the right roles collaborating strongly with each other and with the customer experience at heart. Delays in confronting issues that arise in product business management are costly.

7. Implement a nine-box talent management tool

A process that works very well for getting focus on the quality of talent in an organisation or team is the nine-box matrix of performance and potential. Creating the matrix requires the performance and potential of each individual to be assessed on an annual basis at least.

A six-monthly review is preferable.

Step 1: Assign a performance — potential rating

Starting at the top of the company, ask people leaders to give each of their direct reports a rating of their individual performance and potential. A rating scale that works is High, Medium or Low.

Step 2: Plot each team's talent onto the matrix

Plot each individual into the nine-box matrix (figure 14.2) based on their rating. At this stage a conversation between the manager doing the ratings with their manager to review their team's matrix is important to make sure they are broadly aligned.

		Potential		
		Low	Medium	High
Performance	**High**	#7	#8	#9
	Medium	#4	#5	#6
	Low	#1	#2	#3

Figure 14.2: nine-box matrix

Step 3: Aggregate ratings to enable peer review

For each level of the organisation, have the HR team compile the ratings of the people leaders onto one matrix so the aggregated results of the distribution (number and percentage of the population) in the nine boxes can be reviewed.

For example, the direct reports of the CEO should sit together to review and discuss the rolled-up ratings of all their direct reports, to calibrate across functions of the business and to ensure feedback is shared by their peers.

Step 4: Review key trends

If this isn't the first time you are doing the exercise, compare the current distribution with the last time the exercise was run.

If the management team is strengthening, the number and percentage of people in segments #1, #2, #3 and #4 will be decreasing and the number and percentage of people in segments #5, #6, #7, #8 and #9 will be increasing.

The process serves as a reminder of the need to address, or performance manage, people in the low performance box of the matrix.

Step 5: Commit to action

Put action plans in place to performance manage people rated as low performing, especially those who have received this rating more than once. Make sure the #9s are being promoted and challenged with bigger roles and further development opportunities.

This exercise turns quality of management and individual talent into data that can be analysed and discussed and be the focus of ongoing attention.

An important part of this process is the opportunity it provides management teams to review the performance of people in their peers' departments. This calibration helps drive a consistent and more objective performance conversation and focus across the organisation, because more perspectives are gained from the discussion.

It is important to call out that this process can be confronting for teams that have not done it before. The process depends on a commitment to confidentiality, so that any opinions expressed about an individual are not shared outside the room by anyone other than the manager of the person concerned.

This process helps draw performance issues to the surface and create accountability of each manager to address the issues of performance in their teams. It also helps identify the best talent and to enable a discussion about advancement and development opportunities that may be available for them across the business.

8. Career counselling process

For people in need of help with the hard choices of what to do in the next stage of their career, the following questions and directions are designed to help align head, gut and heart to guide them along potential pathways.

The process involves answering the following questions:

1. Your strengths and areas for development:

    a) Strengths: What do you think they are?

    b) Areas for development: What do you think they are?

2. What you love and don't like about work:

    a) What do you love/want to have in your work life?

    b) What do you dislike/want to avoid in your work life?

3. Reflect on answers to 1 and 2:

    a) What conclusions can you draw from the above four questions?

4. Looking forward what is most important to you?

    a) Informed by the reflections in question 3, in descending order of importance, write down the decision criteria for your next career move.

5. Pathways:

    a) Write down the different potential pathways that are open to you, or those you want to pursue.

6. Rate each of the pathways (low/medium/high) as a fit against each of the following considerations:

    a) your decision criteria in question 4

    b) how accessible it is to you — do you have contacts that you can leverage?

    c) how much learning do you need to pursue it — does the pathway involve some form of study or training?

7. Given the overall ratings in question 6, which of the pathways look best?

8. Write down an action plan for the next 30 days to pursue this pathway — for example:

   a) meeting people who can connect you to potential opportunities

   b) doing further research and/or learning relevant to the pathway

   c) making it happen!

Have someone you trust review what you have written and question you about your thinking and what's behind it. Objective input on questions 3 onwards is valuable.

CHAPTER 15

THE JOURNEY IS THE REWARD

At a Morgan Stanley SaaS Industry CEO conference I attended in 2022, Keith Block, former President of Salesforce, commented that these were the toughest times to be a CEO. So why do it?

The answer is that the work can be incredibly rewarding and a lot of fun.

You might think I mean financially rewarding, and for some that might be the case. For me it's the fun and reward of working closely with a team of people you love to overcome challenges and have helped grow and develop their careers. I've been rewarded in this way many times: people I have worked with have expressed appreciation for the positive impact I have had on their work experience, careers and life. To know you have had a positive influence on others is the ultimate reward for doing the hard work each Must-Do demands.

There's also the feeling of accomplishment when you have taken a business idea and turned it into something special that delivers positive benefits to those it serves, or taken an organisation or team to a higher level of performance and feeling that difference.

Working with great people

I have been incredibly fortunate to meet and work with many talented leaders from different backgrounds and walks of life. When I share my experiences over the past 40 years, I am often asked about the high-profile leaders I've worked with.

One highlight was the opportunity to collaborate with academics, government, business and union leaders during my time as President of the Society for Knowledge Economics (SKE), a not-for-profit think tank that operated from 2005 to 2014. SKE aimed to encourage and promote new and better leadership and management practices that enable innovation, productivity and sustainability.

Other highlights include the opportunity to work with and learn from world class Board Chairs, Catherine Livingstone and John Mullen, during nine years on the Board of Telstra, and Graham Smith and David Thodey during my tenure as CEO of Xero. David and I go way back to the early years at IBM, and I have tremendous respect for what he has accomplished and how he has gone about it.

It has been rewarding to meet, observe and work with leaders who have been at the forefront of the shifts and shocks of the past several decades. Not surprisingly, people often ask me about Steve Jobs, Rod Drury, James Packer, Kerry Packer, Bill Gates and Steve Ballmer. Here is a bit of insight on when and where I crossed paths with these global leaders.

Steve Jobs

Steve Jobs did not shy away from difficult conversations and was comfortable making hard choices. He was in a league of his own in his ability to provide clarity of purpose, priorities and focus.

Several of my encounters with Steve are described elsewhere in this book and each encounter was memorable. He had a way of burning his words or message into your brain.

Shortly after he became interim CEO, Steve brought together regional subsidiary leaders to meet with him and hear what his plans were for the company. We were excited by the opportunity and took notes to capture the key points. He didn't like us writing notes and said in a raised voice, 'You guys are giving me the shits. If you aren't smart enough to remember what I'm telling you, you shouldn't be here.'

Suffice to say, half a dozen pens were quietly placed on the table.

I most enjoyed a one-on-one conversation we had to discuss the various markets in the Asia Pacific region and where it made sense for Apple to compete. I pushed Steve hard on the need for Apple to compete in the lower-priced segment of the market, and to that point he made it clear to me that competing there would only make sense if we could do it with beautiful products. He was kind in his interest and advice.

It's remarkable now to reflect on those days and to see how successful Apple became through the second coming of Steve Jobs and beyond under Tim Cook's leadership.

Steve is testament to the fact that leadership character is not about personality or style. It's about the substance of the work leaders do and the Must-Dos described in this book. Whether you liked the way he treated people or not, Steve was a master of most elements of what it takes to lead change.

Rod Drury

A great reward on my journey was the opportunity to work with Rod Drury, the founder of Xero. My connection with Rod started 10 years before I became CEO when a mutual contact reached out to see if I could help find someone to lead Xero Australia. It was 2010 and I'd recently returned to Australia after working with Microsoft in Seattle. At that time, Xero had revenues of around $10 million with 36 000 subscribers — less than 1 per cent of the scale of Xero today.

Rod needed a leader with good corporate experience and a rebel start-up character — not an easy combination to find — but I had a good person in mind. I recommended Chris Ridd, known well to me at Microsoft Australia, and Rod soon hired him. Chris was a great fit for the Xero opportunity and ultimately one of Rod's most crucial hires in establishing Xero's success in Australia.

In 2016, my second encounter with Xero was at the request of another former Microsoft connection of mine, Trent Innes, then Xero Australia's Managing Director, who succeeded Chris Ridd. Trent asked me to facilitate a team planning session to help him establish clear and aligned objectives.

Not long after working with Trent I was introduced to another of Rod's great hires, Rachael Powell, Xero's head of HR at the time. Rachael was keen for me to meet Rod and provide similar support to the Xero global leadership team that I provided Trent and the Australian team.

I met up with Rod at the Sydney Hilton hotel shortly after. We agreed that a good starting point would be for me to interview the top 25 Xero leaders and from their feedback make recommendations about how Xero could scale and achieve its aspirations to be a global technology company.

We framed up a change program called Project Infinity and agreed that as part of developing the associated work streams I would facilitate the quarterly Xero leadership team meetings.

From that point, during late 2016, Rod delegated the chair of Xero's quarterly leadership team meetings to me.

Around January of 2018 we had made progress on Project Infinity; however, my impact as a part-time advisor was limiting. I considered asking Rod if we should frame up my role more formally as a head of strategic transformation or change, but he beat me to the punch when he called me and said, 'Steve, thanks for your help with Infinity. It has made it clear to me that whilst Xero has led innovation in small business accounting, more focus now needs to be on scaling the company to serve more customers and markets around the world. The work of the CEO needs to reflect this new reality by building a cohesive leadership team and developing the right business capabilities and processes. I think I am ready to step aside as CEO.'

I responded by asking Rod, 'Are you sure? This is your baby, and it has come so far. Do you really think you can let it go?'

Rod said, 'Yes, and I also think you are the best person who can do it from the work we have done with Infinity. The Chair (Graham Smith) has kicked off the process to replace me and I think you should throw your hat in the ring.'

I told Rod how much I appreciated his confidence in me and decided to take a few days to decide if I would enter the process. After consulting my partner and other close family and friends, I was encouraged to go for it, and on April 1, 2018, I was appointed CEO of Xero.

The truth is I'd have been crazy not to do it. Xero is special for a bunch of reasons.

Xero's purpose, 'To make life better for people in small business, their advisors and communities around the world', is incredibly motivating to many Xero people who have their roots in a family small business and have grown up watching Mum and Dad 'doing the books' at the kitchen table after hours.

I also loved the passion Xero customers and accounting partners had for the company and its product. Rod and the Xero team had made accounting cool and built a cult-like following, best exemplified by the thousands who turned up to find out about the latest from Xero, and to connect with the accounting community, at Xerocon in Australia, the UK and the US.

The explicit human value of Xero is felt deep in the soul of the company. As founder, Rod had an aspiration that Xero would create a workplace where you could do 'the best work of your life' and be your 'true and authentic self'.

I have often been complimented for the great 'human-centric' culture I built at Xero, but it was Rod as founder and the team he led who created the culture. I was a good custodian of that culture and helped evolve it further as change in our business and operating environment demanded. The human-centric core of the culture did not need to change, because it was aligned with the fundamental care and respect that anyone who goes to work every day wants to experience.

James Packer

James Packer was a very supportive stakeholder in my journey as CEO of ninemsn. From the first time we met, and in every interaction after that, James was always respectful and keen to learn what he could from our time together. He asked a lot of good questions.

James's support of ninemsn against the backdrop of the powerful CEOs at the Nine Network and ACP magazine group was key to making sure we got the support we needed from the owners of the media brands we were extending online.

James and I shared a spreadsheet with five-year revenue and profit projections for ninemsn and occasionally he would ring me to have a chat about how it was shaping up. We both thought ninemsn could have been much bigger than it became.

First, the shareholders (PBL and Microsoft Corp) had very different views on the extent to which ninemsn should diversify or invest into classifieds and other verticals.

While some moves were made by ninemsn, such as the investment in health insurance aggregator iSelect, and an early stake in REA brokered by Brett Chenoweth, our Head of Corporate Development, Microsoft had a limiting view of ninemsn as an online media portal. PBL and James ended up independently participating in other categories, such as very good investments made in Seek and Carsales.

The other reason why ninemsn didn't reach its full potential was Microsoft's difficulties competing in Search. Ninemsn was the clear number one online media property in Australia until 2005, when Google took over that position.

Microsoft saw the strategic opportunity to build a search product and had its own effort underway, but by the time Microsoft started to ship, Google was emerging as the force it ultimately became.

I have great respect for James and his courage to try new things and take the risks associated with being at the forefront of changes in the industry. While he always receives far more coverage for his difficulties than for his successes, he deserves respect for many of his moves in the media industry.

Kerry Packer

Occasionally when I visited James, he would take me into his father's office for a chat. Kerry Packer was a giant in the Australian media and entertainment industry with a formidable reputation and hands-on style with his highly successful media businesses.

On one occasion I presented to the PBL Board and made the mistake of complimenting them on the moves being made to participate in the digital media world, to reduce the impact of industry and technology change on its traditional media business in TV and magazines. Kerry didn't appreciate the compliment and quickly jumped on me: 'Son, it will take a shitload of online advertising to replace the decline in what we generate from 20 minutes out of every hour of television.'

I made that mistake only once and in every other interaction made sure to keep my comments on message.

A highlight of my time at ninemsn was Kerry's attendance at a ninemsn Board meeting. There was no doubting his experience and insight. Kerry often couched his views with a qualification of his limited knowledge of online business, but everything he said made sense — except perhaps his view that, like magazines and newspapers, we needed to make astrology a content centrepiece!

One area where we had a different view to Kerry was on the subject of online media measurement. Rather than do what we were actively doing at the time to promote a standardised online industry audience measurement, Kerry felt that as the leading player at the time, we would be better off not to encourage or engage in standardisation, as it would help our competitors more than us. We were left to contemplate that one.

The biggest gripe Kerry had with ninemsn and Microsoft was how, in his own words, 'Google was beating the shit out of us in Search.'

Kerry was right on that score.

Bill Gates

I had the opportunity to host Bill Gates, Chairman and then Chief Software Architect of Microsoft, during a visit to Australia in 2004. The visit came shortly after Bill handed the role of CEO to Steve Ballmer.

We spent months negotiating with Bill's office on the itinerary, which included meetings with then Prime Minister John Howard and the Leader of the Opposition, Mark Latham.

The briefing book we assembled, under strict instruction from Bill's office, required intricate details of every meeting we had on the agenda. The binder ended up being two and a half inches thick with background details of every person Bill would interact with, along with backgrounds on every government department, customer and NGO that was participating in the program. It took a tremendous amount of planning and work to prepare the agenda, including phone calls to review the program with people in his office.

I first met Bill on the visit when he stepped into the back of a big black SUV that was arranged to transport him from what is now the Four Seasons hotel in Sydney, to dinner with NSW Premier Bob Carr and a group of business and opinion leaders. I was ready for any questions Bill had about the proceedings that night and, given the extent of our briefing document, expected he may have some very specific questions drawn from his pre-reading.

Bill shook my hand as he leaned in the van and then once seated to my left, turned to me and said calmly,

'So, what are we doing?'

I was taken aback, given the amount of detail in our briefing book. It seemed that Bill hadn't read much, if any, of it.

Before each meeting, our modus operandi for the visit involved a short briefing where I would cover who we were meeting, what points I wanted Bill to make, and the issues he might choose to steer clear of. Bill was well versed after years of conducting visits of this kind and handled them very well.

Preparing the briefing document was more about ensuring we had our act together than about Bill being well prepared. Still, it was a useful process even if the purpose was different from what we had expected.

It was clear from the short time I spent with Bill that he was very thoughtful. On one occasion during a quiet lunch break I was speaking with him, without making eye contact, as was often the case. I asked if he would prefer I stop talking and allow him to contemplate. He responded by insisting I should keep talking.

When I escorted Bill to his private jet to depart Australia, he had mounted the stairs to the plane door when he stopped, turned around and descended the stairs to shake my hand, thank me and wish me well.

Steve Ballmer

Steve's tenure as Microsoft CEO has mixed reviews due to Microsoft's relatively flat share price, some missed opportunities and slower revenue growth under his leadership. Despite that view, there was a lot to love about Ballmer's leadership of the company.

His enthusiasm and drive to execute were a high-water mark for any CEO in my experience. Steve was great with customers and always demonstrated a sincere interest in our business around the world. He was always sensitive that Microsoft, as a global company, needed to be led by leaders with local experience and strong cultural links to each market. A significant achievement under Steve's leadership was the transformation of Microsoft to become the leading provider of software to business, government and the largest enterprises — a significant precursor to Microsoft's current success.

It was always fun to have Steve visit Australia, which he did often, and have him share his vision and enthusiasm amongst our people, customers and key stakeholders.

We would also look forward to his appearances at our Global Sales Conferences, where each year he would share the business priorities of the year to come and proclaim 'I love this company!'

The tenure of a CEO should be judged in part by how successful their successor is. Microsoft would not be as successful as it is today without the progress (and learning from mistakes) during the Steve Ballmer era.

Achieving something special

Following founder Rod Drury on the Xero journey is more than a career highlight for me, it's a life highlight. What Rod and many Xero people before me accomplished, along with those on the journey during my time as CEO, was phenomenal.

There were many milestones to celebrate over those seven years. One of my favourites was facilitating the meeting in 2016 where Xero Australia Managing Director Trent Innes outlined his bold ambition to grow Xero Australia to one million subscribers by the end of FY21 — three times the 367 000 Australian subscribers at that time.

Trent's ambition was achieved on schedule in September 2020. It was a special highlight in my time as CEO of Xero, and something Trent and all who supported him are justifiably proud of. Success in Australia has been the foundation of Xero's progress and global ambitions. The reward of our efforts and those who contributed to Xero shine through in table 15.1, which shows the progress during my years working with the company.

Table 15.1: Xero data points, 2016-2023

	FY17	FY23
Number of subscribers	1 035 000	3 741 000
Revenue (M)	$295.4	$1399.9
Annualised recurring (ARR $m)	$359.7	$1553.8
Free cash flow (M)	–$70.8	$102.34
Number of people	1721	5080

The decision to move from a consulting role supporting Rod into the CEO role at Xero was a hard choice at the time. I had just turned 60, was a non-executive director with Telstra and Fletcher Building, and hadn't had an executive role for nine years. My personal life was great and my work/life balance was where I wanted it.

What motivated and excited me about Xero was a belief that the technology industry had underserved small business, the last frontier, for too long. Being able to have a positive impact on the adoption of cloud technology by small business was meaningful to the economy, families and their communities, and something I had to do.

That passion for Xero was never clearer than in my interaction at an Air New Zealand corporate function with a married couple who ran a small business in Wellington. When they asked who I worked for and I answered Xero, the woman said, 'Xero saved our marriage!' I laughed and at that her husband replied, 'She isn't joking!' They went on to describe the nightmare of managing their business before they adopted Xero.

Most of all, the culture of Xero felt like home to me.

The deep care for each other and those Xero does business with comes from Xero's founder, its Kiwi heritage and, more deeply, the connection with Māori and the proverb, *He tangata he tangata he tangata* in reference to what is most important: 'It is people, it is people, it is people!'

Xero as a company, and the leaders and team I worked with, exemplified being human in how we approached our roles and responsibilities, our people, customers and partners. We weren't perfect but we achieved a tremendous amount under challenging circumstances.

FINAL THOUGHTS

I wrote this book to share my experiences at the forefront of major industry shifts and shocks that shaped everything I have learned about leading and responding to change.

The eight Must-Dos represent a way to think and act that can guide you to success and having more fun doing the hard work leaders and their teams need to do in the face of change. It is hard work, because real change happens through difficult conversations, hard choices and tough actions that sometimes impact people close to you.

Your personal level of accountability and commitment is the key factor in determining if you can close the gap between current reality and your aspirations (and those of people around you).

NFL quarterback Tom Brady put it very well in his New England Patriots Hall of Fame induction speech: *'To be successful at anything, the truth is you don't have to be special. You just have to be what most people aren't. Consistent, determined, and willing to work for it. No shortcuts.'*

This book and all the other great books on leadership, teamwork and change can't help you without your commitment to knowing yourself better and willingness to confront difficult conversations and hard choices. That's why at the outset I posed the following question:

How committed are you to prioritise and take action every day that will change things for the better for those around you?

I hope you make that commitment and work hard with people around you to be better every day.

Remember, small steps can make a big difference and doing any one of the following three things each day can become a habit that leads to very positive outcomes.

1. **Think about how you think, by observing yourself in action.**

2. **Do one thing to improve how you and others are working together.**

3. **Have a difficult conversation you might be avoiding.**

I've learned over the years the importance of being willing and able to have difficult conversations and make hard choices in every aspect of life. As the saying goes, 'You are the decisions or choices you make.'

I know for sure that I would have been a better partner and father had I much earlier developed the capability I have today to speak the truth in a respectful and sensitive way, in both my work and my personal life. That said, it is something I am still challenged by and believe is at the core of what makes change a hard process for us humans.

A question sometimes asked is whether leaders are born or made. It is a question that can't be answered conclusively because it seeks to separate two complex and intertwined elements to define how leaders evolve.

In my opinion, no one can be born ready to lead because no one reaches a leadership position without the formative influences and shaping experiences of childhood and youth, surrounded by family, friends and educators.

Character and capability are outcomes of 'being' and 'doing' that evolve from experience with the influence and support of people around us. I give credit for my character and capability to everyone who has contributed to my development as a person and a professional. As they say, 'It takes a village'!

Our future will be framed by how we respond to the shifts and shocks we experience. Pressure will only increase on us to demonstrate the character and capabilities needed to lead and respond to change better as individuals, teams, organisations and nations. In sharing the eight Must-Dos that guide me, I hope I have helped you in some way on the journey of change that lies ahead for you.

I wish you well!

GRATITUDE

Collaborating with Jane O'Connell, who worked with me at ninemsn and played an important role in encouraging me and shaping this book, has been a pleasure and of great help.

Thank you to Lucy Raymond and the team at Wiley for believing in the book and helping make it one I am proud of.

Thank you to the leaders I respect so much who took the time to read the draft manuscript and provide helpful feedback and guidance: David Thodey AO, Tom Daunt, Emeritus Professor Roy Green AM, Professor Leanne Rowe AM, Narelle Hooper, Rachael Powell, Brett Chenoweth, David Do, Christa Davies, David Shein, Sophie Crawford-Jones, John Vamos, Kendra Vant, Cheryl Godkin, Stephanie Avramides, Jamie Pond and Damien Ponweera.

I'm grateful to my parents, Peter and Kathy Vamos, who made me feel like one of the most important people in the world, but never better or more deserving than anyone else in the world. I am very fortunate for having been born and raised in Australia, thanks to my parents' courage.

I'm grateful for the great education I received at Ku-ring-gai High School and the University of New South Wales and for the opportunity to follow my dad's footsteps and join IBM Australia in December of 1979. IBM established many of the standards that have defined the human-centric foundations of the information technology industry.

I'm grateful for the experiences I had working at Apple and Microsoft during challenging times in their history, and to lead ninemsn at the dawn of the digital media age.

Thank you to the many fantastic people I have worked with over the years, especially my teammates at the IBM PC Company, Apple Australia and Asia Pacific, ninemsn, Microsoft Australia and New Zealand, Microsoft Online Services Group, Telstra and most recently the Xero Leadership team. Thanks to Hayley Baines, who supported me in various roles as my Executive Assistant over 15 years.

Thank you to the Xero Board for the opportunity to join Xero, live in New Zealand and lead a global technology company born in the same part of the world as me.

Thanks to my lovely daughters Stephanie Avramides and Flynn Vamos, their mother Karen Vamos and my siblings John Vamos, Michael Vamos and Karen McNeil. Your love and support through the years has helped ground me through the highs and get me through the lows. Also thank you to my brother John, for your inspiration and always sharing with me your knowledge of the human change domain.

Finally, thank you to my beautiful life partner and wife, Cheryl Godkin, for your love, and support in everything I do, including your encouragement and feedback as I wrote this book.

SOURCES

Amelio, Gil (1998). *On the Firing Line: My 500 Days at Apple.*

Dispenza, Joe (2012). *Breaking the Habit of Being Yourself: How to Lose Your Mind and Create a New One.*

Gil, Elad (2018). *The High Growth Handbook.*

Hamel, Gary (2012). *What Matters Now: How to Win in a World of Relentless Change, Ferocious Competition, and Unstoppable Innovation.*

Harris, Robert (2016). *Conclave.*

Isaacson, Walter (2011). *Steve Jobs.*

Keller, Gary W, and Papasan, Jay (2013). *The One Thing: The Surprisingly Simple Truth Behind Extraordinary Results.*

Kerr, James (2015). *Legacy: What the All Blacks Can Teach Us about the Business of Life.*

Lencioni, Patrick (2020). *The Motive: Why So Many Leaders Abdicate Their Most Important Responsibilities.*

Lencioni, Patrick (1994). *The Five Dysfunctions of a Team: A Leadership Fable.*

LePera, Nicole (2021). *How to Do the Work: Recognize Your Patterns, Heal from Your Past, and Create Your Self.*

Maté, Gabor (2022). *The Myth of Normal: Trauma, Illness and Healing in a Toxic Culture.*

Nadella, Satya (2017). *Hit Refresh.*

Nestor, James (2020). *Breath: The New Science of a Lost Art.*

Parrish, Shane (2023). *Clear Thinking: Turning Ordinary Moments into Extraordinary Results.*

Scott, Kim (2019). *Radical Candor: Be a Kick-Ass Boss Without Losing Your Humanity.*

Senge, Peter, Scharmer, C Otto, Jaworski, Joseph, and Flower, Betty Sue (2008). *Presence: Human Purpose and the Field of the Future.*

Sinek, Simon (2009). *Start with Why.*

Sisodia, Rajendra, Wolfe, David, and Sheth, Jagdish N (2007). *Firms of Endearment: How World-Class Companies Profit from Passion and Purpose.*

Sutton, Robert I (2012). *Good Boss, Bad Boss: How to be the Best…and Learn from the Worst.*

Trimboli, Oscar (2022). *How to Listen: Discover the Hidden Key to Better Communication.*

Vamos, John (2022). *Four Voices.*

Werbach, Adam (2009). *Strategy for Sustainability: A Business Manifesto.*

Wilde, Kevin D (2022). *Coachability: The Leadership Superpower.*